THE COMPLETE BOOK OF
SMALL ANTIQUES COLLECTING

Katharine M. McClinton

THE COMPLETE BOOK
OF
Small Antiques
Collecting

COWARD - McCANN, Inc.
NEW YORK

TO HAY

MY MOST PRECIOUS ANTIQUE

RARE, EXPENSIVE, NOT AVAILABLE

Contents

Contents

V *Antiques for the Epicure*

VI *Victoriana*

Introduction

Antique collecting has become an important hobby for many Americans. Preferences range from such inexpensive items as bottles, souvenir spoons, pressed or fancy glassware, cut glass, mechanical banks and match safes to expensive eighteenth-century silver and china.

Nothing is too small or too unimportant for the enthusiastic collector. Some people collect what appeals to their fancy but the really smart collector specializes. If he has considerable money to invest, he buys from a reliable dealer and takes the dealer's advice. But many collectors relish the adventure of searching in smaller shops and out-of-the-way places, and prefer to learn by their own mistakes. However, if he is a serious collector he should know something about what he is collecting and learn to recognize and evaluate an antique. There are several ways of learning.

First of all, he should visit all the antique shows possible. There are large and important shows in each section of the country, such as the Armory Show in New York, the White Plains Show and the Connecticut shows managed by Russell Carrel. There are also the Annual Antique Show in Fort Lauderdale, Florida, and the shows in Pasadena and Riverside, California, and Phoenix, Arizona, managed by Jean

Woodruff, but there are also dozens of small antique shows held for charity and church benefits. In the East most shows are held in the autumn or the spring. In the winter the shows are seen in Florida, Arizona and California.

Browsing in antique shops is another way of learning about antiques. There are also antique village restorations scattered throughout the country which show the antique in its proper setting.

I

Country Antiques

Country antiques in the home of Mr. and Mrs. Ben Prins. PHOTO,
EZRA STOLLER, COURTESY MC CALL'S MAGAZINE.

American Weather Vanes, Decoys and Eagles

W EATHER VANES and decoys have natural associations with country living, and a collection of either may be used in the indoor or outdoor decoration of a home in the country. The cock is the best-known weather-vane emblem. In the nineteenth century, a papal decree made the cock the symbol for the Christian Church weather vane. In Europe, no church was without its weathercock, and the churches of early America followed the tradition. The early European ones are of wrought iron. Early hand-wrought iron weather vanes had iron spiral designs with initials and date or a motto cut in the iron banner.

The weather vane from the Old Mill in Chester, Pennsylvania, has initials and the date 1699. The wrought-iron vane on Independence Hall in Philadelphia has a Liberty cap, wings and an arrow. Dated weather vanes also have crowns, sailing ships and fish. The rare iron vane at Moravian Seminary in Bethlehem, Pennsylvania, has an Agnus Dei with the word HEYL cut in the banner which the lamb holds. Other eighteenth-century iron weather vanes in Pennsylvania have cocks and tulips. Later American weather vanes were cut out of sheet iron, copper or zinc. Examples of these early copper cock weather vanes are still to be seen on New England church steeples. The earliest cocks are simple silhouette cut-outs with angular outlines and holes for eyes. Later they were embossed and more realistic, showing wings and feathers. Roosters were also made in polychromed wood.

The first known American weather-vane maker was Shem Drowne, who fashioned the copper cock which is now on the First Church in Cambridge, Massachusetts. Drowne also made the grasshopper with green-glass eyes on the cupola of Faneuil Hall, Boston, Massachusetts.

In the nineteenth century this design was copied by L. W. Cushing and Sons, of Waltham, Massachusetts, and these vanes are sought by collectors. Other early weather-vane designs include the Indian with his bow and arrow, the horse, the fish, the snake, the whale, the angel Gabriel and the eagle. The variety of these simple contours shows the ingenuity of the early American craftsman. The technique of his craft controlled his design and made for its direct and spontaneous expression. The fact that the weather vane was to be seen from a distance put emphasis on its outline, and there was no reason to add detail which could not be seen or which would inhibit its function.

By the midnineteenth century, weather vanes were made in large numbers. They were still cut in sheet-metal silhouette or carved in wood by local artisans, but they were also made commercially. Weather vanes had become a thriving industry and were manufactured in factories in New York and other eastern states. By this time there were many new designs, and the catalogues of the period show horses, cows, sheep, pigs and scenes with several figures such as a horse and colt, a man driving a pig or plowing. For seacoast villages there were weather vanes with ships, sailors, sea gulls and various kinds of fish. There were also the racing trotters or jockeys on horseback, pheasants, peacocks, ostriches, pigeons, squirrels, deer, locomotives and steamboats. Patriotic weather vanes included the Goddess of Liberty, Columbia, the American eagle, Uncle Sam and a Revolutionary soldier.

Weather vanes also took on the duty of a commercial sign, and the fireman or the fire engine on the weather vane located the firehouse; the pig and the butcher, the slaughterhouse; and the ram, the woolen mill. Some quaintly shaped carved wooden figures had moveable arms which whirled with the breeze. These were called whirligig weather vanes. They were painted in several colors. Such subjects as "Sailor Jack," the British soldier or the "Gentleman" were made around 1840 and must be unique pieces.

In 1853 Isaiah Washburne established E. G. Washburne & Company in New York City. The firm made the weather vanes on St. Paul's Church and the New York City Hall, and in the early twentieth century those for many big estates on Long Island. The Washburne weather vanes were made of hand-hammered copper and covered with gold leaf. The designs included arrows and banners, and eagles, horses and cows. The company is still making weather vanes in the shape of arrows and trotting horses, as well as special custom designs.

Much of the charm of old weather vanes comes from the techniques used by the makers. Except for the cast-iron pieces, even the commercial vanes were finished by hand. Wooden vanes were cut out with small saws and carved with a chisel. Weather vanes of wood were usually painted

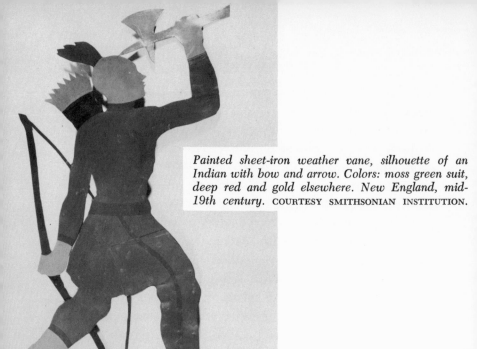

Painted sheet-iron weather vane, silhouette of an Indian with bow and arrow. Colors: moss green suit, deep red and gold elsewhere. New England, mid-19th century. COURTESY SMITHSONIAN INSTITUTION.

Carved wooden weather-vane figure for a butcher shop, c. 1815.
COURTESY SMITHSONIAN INSTITUTION.

to protect them from the weather. White, Indian red or yellow were the most popular colors. Some weather vanes were painted in several colors and some were polychromed or gilded. Copper vanes were left unpainted and the old ones are usually green with age.

Weather vanes are not plentiful but there are enough in shops and at antique shows to make the hunt interesting. They are not marked. You must educate your eye to recognize the early designs; the later ones can be identified by referring to the pages of old catalogues.

DECOYS

Decoys are models of wild fowl—duck, geese and other birds—which were carved and painted to deceive live birds and lure them within range of the hunter's gun. Although they were made for a practical utilitarian purpose, decoys are carved with such direct simplicity that they rate as folk carving. They are one form of folk art that existed in Colonial days and still continues to the present, although in the latter part of the nineteenth century and even today they are made in factories in great quantities. Decoys were made by hunters, carpenters and whittlers, as well as by the professional decoy carver.

The techniques and materials of decoymaking have changed little through the years. There are several types. Those carved in the round from a solid block of white pine or cedar are made to float. The flat, profile "stick-up" decoy is attached to a stick so that it can be stuck in the grass marshes where the birds come for seeds. These two types are the most decorative and thus most desirable to the average collector.

Stick-up decoys were the earliest type. They include the blue heron, plover, snipe, dowitcher and other shore birds, and the wild pigeon.

Carved wood solid decoys are made in two parts, the body and the head. Those made in the factory are turned on the lathe but the heads and tails are finished by hand. The heads of the hand-carved decoys are given a final finish with a jackknife after the head and body are assembled. Then the decoy is sandpapered and painted. The eyes are carved or painted or of glass. Old decoys were painted in solid colors, but some new ones show realistic feathers.

Different kinds of decoys are used in hunting wild fowl, and decoys differ in various regions. Some are characteristic of New England, Long Island, Chesapeake Bay, the Gulf States and other parts of the country, so there are many types that might be assembled by the serious collector. In addition to the wide variety, decoys are available in considerable quantity and at comparatively reasonable prices. They are not only interesting and decorative, but they are worth collecting as American folk art.

A good specimen should show the essential characteristics of the bird represented. Even the characteristics of various types of ducks have a distinction. The male eider duck is stolid and heavy, while the pintail has more flowing lines. The swan is of course the most graceful of all fowl. The long, flat-shaped loon has a button tail and a sedate appearance. Plovers and other shore birds are more slender.

A decoy is judged from the grace of its outline, which should be as simple and primitive as modern sculpture. The painting and condition of the decoy are also important to the collector. The list of decoy ducks gives an alluring pic-

New England painted sign. Early 19th century. COURTESY GINSBURG & LEVY, INC.

Decoy shore birds. PHOTO, EZRA STOLLER, COURTESY MC CALL'S MAGAZINE.

Decoy duck. American, 19th century. PHOTO, EZRA STOLLER, COURTESY MC CALL'S MAGAZINE.

ture. In addition to the mallard and canvasback there are the pintail, and the black, ruddy and redhead duck, the eider and the broadbill, the wood and the bufflehead. Of birds, there are blue heron, drake, quail, pigeon, teal, swan, crane, robin and loon.

EAGLES

The American eagle is one of the most sought after collector's items. Wooden, iron and earthenware eagles are decorative and attractive to place over the doorway of a country house or on the wall above the fireplace. Eagle door knockers give interest to the front door. There are a great many varieties of American eagle designs, and the story of the insignia has close connection with the many channels of our national and private life through the centuries.

The choice of the eagle as the American patriotic symbol was made in 1782. Several prominent men had a part in the selection and in the details of the final design. William Rush, the well-known sculptor of Philadelphia, wrote his suggestions to the committee selecting the design of figureheads for naval vessels. He said, "It ought to be an elegant figure. The American Eagle darting upon and destroying the vitals of tyranny, the shackles of despotism . . . and hurling them under the feet of the Genius of America."

However, Charles Thomson and William Barton shaped the form of the eagle seal of the United States, and two designs were rejected before the final seal design was accepted. It was they who decided that it should not be the eagle of heraldry but the American or bald eagle. The seal design shows the eagle with outspread wings, holding arrows

Textile, War of 1812, showing eagle symbol. COURTESY NEW YORK
HISTORICAL SOCIETY.

in one claw and an olive branch in the other, and a crest with thirteen stars. This seal was adopted June 20, 1782, and from that time on the eagle in one form or another has been popular in America.

On Washington's triumphal tour he was greeted everywhere by painted and carved eagles. Eagles were always popular in American folk art. After the eagle became the national emblem, it appeared as a design in many different ways and in many different materials and techniques. It was carved on ship's figureheads, where it was a bald eagle with spread wings and open talons, with or without the shield of stars and stripes. The eagle was scratched on powder horns. It was put on weather vanes and shop signs, carved and gilded for flagpoles, and even used in appliqué or woven on quilts.

In the Federal period the eagle was used as an architectural motif and was carved over doorways and mantelpieces by Samuel McIntire and others. It was also carved and inlaid on furniture of the period and mounted on clocks. Women embroidered eagle emblems with gold thread and bright silk. During the War of 1812 cotton printed kerchiefs showed the eagle emblem in a design together with scenes of naval battles and portraits of Washington and Jefferson. Any patriotic celebration such as the Erie Canal ceremonies in 1825 brought forth souvenirs which usually had an eagle emblem. A water keg in the New York Historical Society has a painted eagle used in the Erie Canal ceremonies. Fire engines, fire signals and fire-fighting equipment such as buckets and hats were often decorated with eagles.

Eagles have always been a favorite design for glassware. Early engraved glasses and decanters often have this emblem. When Lafayette visited America in 1824-1825, at least five

Carved wooden eagle, J. Bowers, 1861. COURTESY NEW YORK HISTORICAL SOCIETY.

Carved wooden eagle from door-way of Eagle Hotel, Bronx, 1880. COURTESY NEW YORK HISTORICAL SOCIETY.

Carved wooden eagle. Wilhelm Schimmel (1817–1890). COURTESY NEW YORK HISTORICAL SOCIETY.

different glassworks made flasks which included eagles on one side. Continuing through the years, the eagle flask has been a favorite with collectors, and dozens of different kinds in various colors and designs exist. Eagles are also found on many pressed-glass cup plates and salts. There are also milk-glass covered dishes with spread eagles on their covers. Eagles were printed on wallpaper designs for bandboxes and woven into coverlets in the midnineteenth century. These coverlets with eagle seal designs, stars, and patriotic mottoes can be seen in the Smithsonian Institution, and one of the most striking, marked 1853, was recently given to the San Diego Museum of Fine Arts.

Patriotic china also has many eagle motifs. Both Staffordshire and china made in America used the emblem. Early pottery eagles were made at Bennington and in Pennsylvania and Ohio potteries. Eagle butter molds and trivets are the least expensive of these items. There are many early engraved trade cards with eagle motifs. Eagles made as ships' figureheads, for flagpoles or for doorways, are the most expensive and the most difficult to find. Schimmel and Mount eagles of any size are expensive, as are those carved by John Bellamy, Henry Purrington or any other well-known carver.

American Hinges, Latches, Locks and Keys

A^{N} IRON FOUNDRY was established in Saugus, Massachu-setts, in 1644, but much of the ironwork continued to be brought over from England. However, there were blacksmiths in America and many came as bond servants, according to a notice in the New York *Gazette,* June 10, 1728. There were even blacksmiths listed among the trades-men of the seventeenth century.

Hinges of all sorts, padlocks and spring locks were evi-dently considered a necessity in early America, and among those listed in the Boston *Gazette* on August 2, 1756 were: "Stock locks, egg nob locks, and other door locks, "H" and "HL" hinges, pew hinges, hooks and hinges, and garrets, chest hinges, door latches." The first Boston blacksmith re-corded in early newspapers was William Bryant, mentioned in the Boston *News Letter* on July 6, 1732. Robert Hendry, "Blacksmith and locksmith . . . Horse Shoer also all sorts of locks are made and mended," advertised in the Boston *Gazette* on December 10, 1751. There were also blacksmiths in New York, although such articles as "Locks and hinges of all sorts and sizes" were advertised by Peter Goelet, "At the Sign of the Golden Key," and Peter T. Curtenius, "At the Sign of the Golden Anvil and Hammer," in the New York newspapers of the 1760's as just being imported from England. Robert Boyd, Blacksmith, had a "shop near the Old English Church" in New York in 1760. In the *Royal Gazette*, September 19, 1778, we read that Alexander Smith, "At the Sign of the Lock, Jack and Bell—makes, repairs and cleans locks and keys, and all sorts of Jacks and Hinges," and in 1782 James Kip is "making keys for door and chest locks."

In the small towns the ironworker was generally the village blacksmith, who did everything from shoeing horses to making hinges, locks and keys. In the country, these were often made by the farmer himself or by an itinerant blacksmith who traveled from farm to farm making and mending. Since this service was of such importance in pioneer days, there must have been blacksmiths among the early settlers in each section of the country. This would account for the various foreign influences noticed in the ironwork in different localities. In New England and the larger cities on the east coast the influence of English ironwork was extended by the colonial blacksmith. However, although the English locksmith usually marked his product, few pieces of American ironwork are marked. Also articles such as locks and hinges did not follow the style trends; the same types continued to be made from century to century.

There are many articles of hand-wrought iron for the collector. Builders' hardware would include nails, hasps, hinges, locks and latches. There are also hand-wrought tools such as hammers, gouges, gimlets, tap borers, handsaws, augers, rules and trowels. There are also andirons and fireplace equipment and cooking utensils of hand-wrought iron. Each category has enough items to form a collection. For the householder, latches, hinges, locks and keys are an interesting category, and close to home, for they can be put to useful service or hung on the wall as decoration.

Early latches were hand wrought, whether imported or made in America. They were usually plain but might be decorated with incised lines. American latches were simple and utilitarian, and ornament was handled with restraint. The first American latches were made of oak or hickory wood, and when iron latches were made they often followed the simple design of the wood latch—but of course there were always the English models.

There were four types of Early American wrought-iron latches. The knocker latch was a combination of door knocker and latch; the turning of the knocker opened the latch. The escutcheon plates of these locks are varied in shape: round, square, diamond, heart, hexagonal and octagonal. The knockers also vary in shape from round to elongated. The escutcheon lift latch is the rarest type. It dates from 1797 to 1817, but few examples remain, and they are in museums and not available to collectors. The Suffolk latch is the most interesting of all American latches because it has more variety. The two plates or cusps which fasten to the door are joined by the grasp or central handle. Sometimes these are made of one bar of iron, the plates being hammered or cut out in patterns. The interest in these latches centers on the pattern of the plates. There are many variations in the designs, such as arrowhead, ball and spear, bean, tulip, heart and swordfish. The Pennsylvania Dutch latches were the most elaborate and their cutout designs included hearts, tulips and rare Hessian soldiers. Sometimes the interest centers in the design of the upper plate, and often

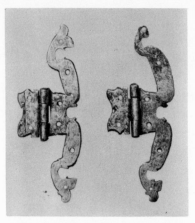

Pair of cock's-head hinges. American, 18th century. COURTESY METROPOLITAN MUSEUM OF ART.

Pair of butterfly hinges. American, 18th century. COURTESY METROPOLITAN MUSEUM OF ART.

Pair of hinges with open heart motif. Pennsylvania, 18th century. COURTESY METROPOLITAN MUSEUM OF ART.

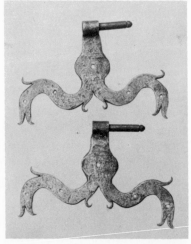

Pair of staghorn hinges. Pennsylvania, 18th century. COURTESY METROPOLITAN MUSEUM OF ART.

there is only one plate. The rare pine tree design was made in Connecticut. Norfolk latches are more common, and the later ones have the plate and handle combined.

Wrought-iron hinges are of various types: the most common and simplest are the "H" and "HL" hinges. These are collectors' items, although not as valuable as the butterfly, ram's-horn or cock's-head hinges. These were not only made for house doors but were also put on barn doors, and there were also hinges on boxes like the old Conestoga wagon toolbox.

Locks and keys can be collected for their aesthetic value, but also for their historic value. They give a history of the industry as well as a picture of the evolution of the lock. The latter purpose was in mind when the Yale and Towne Manufacturing Company assembled its Yale Lock collection. This includes European as well as American locks and keys and shows them from the earliest ages to contemporary times. This collection includes decorative chamberlain keys and other beautiful old keys and locks from Europe.

Designers of locks and keys have always been interested in the esthetic value of their products. The Gothic lock had a V-shaped key guide to help locate the keyhole, but this was retained as a decorative element long after its functional purpose was unnecessary. Also many antique keys such as chamberlain keys were richly decorated because of the custom of wearing them as ornaments to signify ownership and indicate position and authority. Chest locks, although covered from view, are often of intricate workmanship and beauty. This tradition of fine workmanship and aesthetic perfection is reflected in many Early American handmade

American jail padlock and key. Early 19th century.
COURTESY YALE ANTIQUE LOCK COLLECTION.

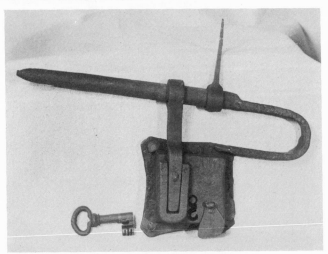

Early 18th-century American door padlock and key, Spanish influence. COURTESY YALE ANTIQUE LOCK COLLECTION.

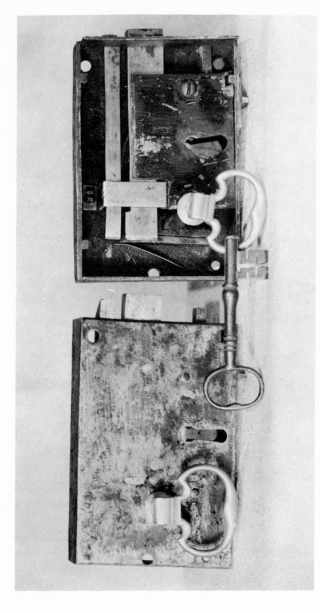

American 18th-century rim locks from descendant of Paul Revere.
COURTESY YALE ANTIQUE LOCK COLLECTION.

locks and keys. Both the handle end and the utilitarian part that fits into the lock have decorative interest. The design of the handle follows decorative styles and sometimes is made up of scroll forms of animal or human figures. The design of the key bit is utilitarian. It is made to fit the lock but even the simplest key bit has a certain beauty.

American eighteenth-century locks include rim and mortise types. Early American keys had simple, flattened oval ring ends and a plain baluster shaft relieved by simple bands of decoration. The key bit is usually cut in a functional pattern. In the nineteenth century, lock inventions were made to increase safety and there were locks with sliding night latches and locks with a percussion cap which fired to frighten an intruder and warn the occupants of the house. In 1858 Yale and Towne memorialized the covered-wagon days in a series of iron padlocks and rim locks called "Westward Ho!" Then there was a small lock that rang a bell when the key was turned, and a large iron executor's lock that required two keys to open. A cast padlock of the 1850 period has a skull-and-bones decorative motif designed to frighten superstitious prowlers. The late nineteenth century also brought a new interest in the design of keys and locks, and designs for keys by well-known artists were often shown in industrial exhibitions in England and France. Undoubtedly many such keys and locks found their way to America and were a part of the hardware of the fine Victorian mansion. One wonders where they are today. Now that Victorian has come to the fore as a major collecting interest, here is one item that could be explored.

The lock collector should understand the mechanism of locks, for this as well as the workmanship often helps to date the lock. Keys can be evaluated by their design and workmanship. There are seldom any marks on old American iron, but a study of the record of old forges and factories might aid in establishing the date and place of manufacture of many articles.

American Cake and Pudding Molds and Cooky Cutters

POTTERY MOLDS for cakes and puddings were at first imported from England and the Continent, but early in the nineteenth century they were made in American potteries located in Vermont, Connecticut, New York, New Jersey, Pennsylvania and Ohio. The best-known pottery molds were made at Bennington, Vermont, although Ohio brownware molds are often taken for "Bennington." Pottery cake, pudding and jelly molds were made in cream, buff, yellow, brown or red earthenware. Often there is a contrasting glaze inside. In shape they are round, oval, oblong and melon. A round, fluted cake mold with a cone center is known as a "turk's head." The mold designs include fruit such as grapes and pineapple; vegetables such as corn; animals, flowers and geometric patterns. Molds usually stand on a base, and the oldest are often set on three legs.

Pudding molds were also made in tin. The sides of tin molds are fluted and the panels have geometrical markings, while the design on the bottom is similar to that on the pottery molds—birds, fruit, vegetables or flowers. These molds are usually oval in shape, but the round "turk's-head" sponge-cake, spiral, fluted molds are to be found. Turk's-head molds were also made in copper.

The Pennsylvania German custom of cooky making at holiday time has given us a fascinating collection of cooky cutters. At Christmas in Pennsylvania Dutch country there is an orgy of baking gingerbread figures and cookies, honey cakes and springerle. The cookies and cakes are hung on the Christmas tree as decoration. In Europe the cutters had been made of hand-carved wood, but since there were few skilled carvers in America, tin was substituted. These whimsical articles of the local tinsmith's craft were made in an infinite variety of shapes of quaint birds, beasts and men.

There are several categories of subject matter for the collector of tin cookie cutters. There are mounted horsemen and forms of men and pantaletted children in enough quantity and diversity to make a collection. The historical figures, which of course are rare and valuable, include such figures as a Revolutionary soldier, a Colonial horseback rider with his three-cornered hat, William Penn with a gigantic peace pipe, and figures of Indian men and women. Later figures included the farmer, the forty-niner, Uncle Sam and the Mennonite woman. There are also fat men, preachers, dwarfs, dandies and baseball players. Another category includes household articles of every kind—top hats, bow ties, pipes, shoes, boots, bowls, bottles, pitchers, axes, guns, pistols and daggers. Animals are numerous and are an especially interesting field for the collector. The domestic kind include horses in great variety and sizes; sheep, goats, pigs, donkeys, cats and dogs of all kinds. Barnyard fowl include the duck, goose, rooster, hen, and the scarcer peacock, turkey, swan and pigeon. Wild animals include the lion, deer, bear, fox,

Mold with frog, yellow glaze. Mid-19th century. COURTESY NEW YORK HISTORICAL SOCIETY.

"Turk's-head" mold. Red earthenware with dark-brown glaze. COURTESY NEW YORK HISTORICAL SOCIETY.

Melon-shaped jelly mold on circular base. Red earthenware with dark-brown splashes in glaze. COURTESY NEW YORK HISTORICAL SOCIETY.

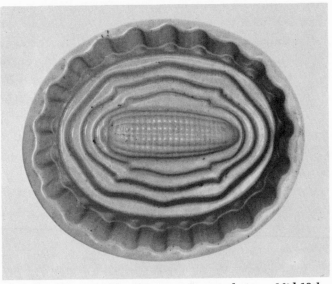

Glazed pottery mold with ear-of-corn design. Mid-19th century. COURTESY NEW YORK HISTORICAL SOCIETY.

skunk, squirrel and rabbit. Camels and hippopotamuses are scarce. There are many birds—swallows, robins, owls, parrots and a rare eagle. There are trees, leaves and flowers of all varieties. The most interesting is the tulip, alone or in a spray with a large central flower and two to four tiny tulips. Then there are four-leaf clovers, half moons, stars and the familiar round-lobed heart.

In size these cutters range from the small 1-inch to large 12-inch horse or the 15-inch gingerbread man. Cooky cutters are not marked. However, the housewife herself often scratched her own name on a cutter, such as "Lettie's Cutter" or "Maria Stohler." Sometimes the cutters were homemade, but more often the itinerant tinsmith traveled from house to house, making the cutters from scraps of tin. Each housewife usually had a whole string of different shaped cutters. A collection of cooky cutters makes an interesting wall decoration for the kitchen or family room, and you may want to use them for your own cookies from time to time.

Cooky molds known as springerle molds for decorating flat cakes are also from Pennsylvania. These may consist of a single design, but usually there are sections of 6, 8 or 24 separate designs all carved in detail with a border around each pattern. The average springerle board consists of 8 designs. They include flowers, cherries and leaves, a bird, a hen on a nest, a house or castle. These boards are about an inch thick and are made of fine-grained hardwood. They are also made of tin. Sometimes the designs were carved on rolling pins, with 8 or 16 designs. Such rolling pins are made commercially today. There were also small, carved individual cake molds.

Marzipan molds of wood, metal, slate or pottery cut in

Tin block for making springerle. American, 19th century.
COURTESY HENRY FORD MUSEUM.

Mahogany cake board. Intaglio Inscription: "Lafayette/
Yorktown/ 1781/ W. Farron." COURTESY NEW YORK
HISTORICAL SOCIETY.

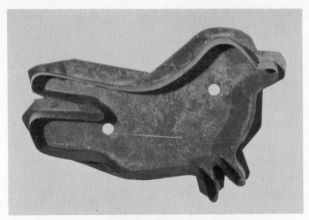

Bird-design tin cooky cutter. American, 19th century. COURTESY NEW YORK HISTORICAL SOCIETY.

Leaf-and-flower tin cooky cutters. American, 19th century.

decorative forms were made in America in the nineteenth century. Many of these had historic, religious or memorial subject matter. In New York before 1830, special celebration molds were made in mahogany, and the names are known of several bakers who made them, or at least made the marzipan which was molded on the boards. These cake celebration molds are rectangular mahogany boards from 14″ to 30″ long. The oval shaped center is intaglio-carved with such subjects as early fire engines. One is marked MANHATTAN, another SUPERIOR. One board in memory of the defeat of Cornwallis is marked YORKTOWN 1781, W. FARRON. The cake-boards in the New York Historical Society include a design of Lafayette mounted on a horse. The design is enclosed within a border of stars and stripes. It is inscribed, LAFAY-ETTE/YORKTOWN/1781/W. FARRON. William Farron was listed as a baker in New York from 1815 through 1835. Needless to say, this board is unique, as is the one inscribed, BRI-TANNIA, GREECE, AMERICA—which commemorates Greece being recognized as a republic. All such American marzipan celebration molds are undoubtedly in museum collections, but similar large European cakeboards are to be found with various designs and subject matter.

Tinware – Plain, Punched and Grocery-Store Tin

E DWARD PATTERSON is credited with establishing the first
manufactory of tinware in America at Berlin, Connecticut, in 1770. The Pattersons, like most tinworkers, peddled
their wares in baskets, on horseback and in wagons. The
itinerant peddler set out in the spring and toured the countryside of New England, Pennsylvania, New York, along the
Ohio Valley and as far down the Mississippi as New Orleans.
He peddled pots, pans, ovens, cups, plates, dippers, candle
molds and candlesticks. His wagon was usually painted red,
and he announced his arrival with a blast on his tin horn.
The tinworker also did repairs and carried his tools in a tin
case with drawers and a flap lid. The tools included hammers, a planishing hammer, plyers, calipers and a soldering
iron. There were also tinsmiths in New York and other
American cities in the late eighteenth century.

In the New York *Gazette and Weekly Mercury*, Septem-
ber 8, 1777, Edward Smith advertises for "Tin-Plate Workers
—Also a few dozen of camp dishes and plates." Andrew
Coughlan, "Tin-Plate Worker," advertised in the New York
Royal Gazette, February 28, 1778: "Camp Plates, oval dishes,

Tinware teapot. American, 19th century. COURTESY HENRY FORD MUSEUM.

Top left: Tin coffeepot, made in Pennsylvania c. 1830 by J. Ketterer. Punched design and initials "J.Y. and H.Y." COURTESY NEW YORK HISTORICAL SOCIETY.

Left: American tin oven. Early 19th century. COURTESY METROPOLITAN MUSEUM OF ART.

American tin lantern, 19th century. COURTESY METROPOLITAN MUSEUM OF ART.

American tin lantern, 18th century. COURTESY METROPOLITAN MUSEUM OF ART.

soup pots, stew-pans, tureens, soup ladles, japanned punch jugs, canteens, tumblers, tea pots, furnished candlesticks, tea urns, waiters, tea chests, canisters and coffee jugs, India Patterns." This tin may have been imported from England, since we know that there was even a scarcity of tin canteens and kettles for the Revolutionary Army.

In the New York *Gazette and Weekly Mercury,* September 3, 1781, Samuel Kempton, "Tin-Plate Worker," and Robert Easton, "Tinman," both advertise the "newly constructed Salisbury Kitchens for baking, boiling, and roasting at the same time." Kempton also states in an ad in 1785 that "he has on Hand, a very large and extensive assortment of all kinds of Tin, Copper, Brass and Jappanned wares," and as he manufactures the most of the articles, he is determined that "none shall undersell" him.

"The Conjurer" (quick cooker) was another cooking vehicle which, together with an "Improved Roasting Oven," was advertised by D. Crawley of New York in 1797. "The Improved Roasting Oven does the basting on the top by means of a hopper and strainer which causes the fat to drip gradually on the victuals roasting." In 1799, August Parise of New York advertised: "Tin and Copper bathing conveniences . . . Also Bidets and Syringes." From these ads we can see that America of even Revolutionary days was beginning to get some of the conveniences of the Continent.

For the kitchen there were all sizes of pots, measures, teakettles, skillets, spiders, roasters, frying pans and Dutch ovens. The first roasting oven was called the Tin Kitchen. It was half cylindrical in shape and stood on four feet. A spit held the meat, and a small door at the back was used for basting. Sometimes these ovens have perforated initials on the door. Skewers to help hold the meat on the spit were of iron and kept on by hand-hammered holders. These sets of skewers can be found today; the ovens of course are rare. There were also several types of biscuit ovens constructed on the same principle as the roasting ovens. Plate warmers were of several types; the small one called a tin bonnet, and the larger one set on legs. There were tin gridirons, corn poppers and coffee-bean roasters. When stoves came into use, utensils for the top of the stove, such as teakettles, were made.

There were also many small articles of household usage, such as strainers and graters. Graters made of pierced tin had various patterns of dots, dashes and circles. Strainers usually had a wooden rim. Sausage guns and choppers, milk pans, butter churns, various kinds of whippers, rolling pins and pie crimpers, skimmers, cooky cutters and pudding molds are also items for the collector. But the most decorative and useful items were the various candlesticks, lanterns and chandeliers. There were small candlesticks and chamber candlesticks with a saucer. Trays and snuffers, a candlebox and candle molds were all necessary accessories. The candle molds were made for one candle and as many as twenty-four or more. They were of various types. Those arranged in a circle with a saucer and cone top are rare.

Candle shields and wall sconces are of various patterns. With the invention of matches, tin matchboxes were made and many types of tin Betty Lamps were in use. Lucius Hart, who had been in partnership with the Boardmans, makers of pewter and Britanniaware in New York City since about 1831, purchased the entire stock of the firm in 1847, and soon afterward advertised tinware for sale: "Foot warmers, bed warmers and lanterns."

Lanterns were of various types. Round, pierced tin lanterns with cone tops are the most common. They have panels of pierced tin on their sides and tops. The rectangular lanterns with glass panels and a pierced tin dome, such as the celebrated Paul Revere lantern in the Concord Antiquarian Society, are rare. After the Civil War tinware was in even more demand, and with the rise of the railroads, the railroad lantern with its red and green glass windows was a common item of tinware, although the first railroad lamps were only an oilcan with a spout for a wick. There was also a wide variety of other small lamps—the miner's lamp, lamps for whaling vessels, the nurses' lamp, the rare Bible-reading lamp and the table lamp with tiny crimped or molded shade. Tin matchboxes with a top that could not be opened by mice were patented in 1864. There were also wall cases for comb and brush.

The coffeepot with sectioned gooseneck spout is usually credited to the Pennsylvania Dutch. These pots were decorated with punched designs of tulips, birds, hex signs and hearts. Sometimes they had initials or a maker's name such as "Uebele" or "Shade." On top of the lid was a brass finial. These pots date between 1830 and 1850. They were made of many pieces, fitted and soldered together, the handle and spout separately attached. All pots are the same shape. There were also pots with ribbed designs, pitchers, and chocolate and teapots.

A patent for tin cans was taken out by Peter Durrand in 1810, and in 1819, Thomas Rensett of New York and William Underwood of Boston were advertising tin-can containers. Berries and tomatoes were canned in tins as early as 1821, and Borden's Milk sold in tins in 1856. But the tin packages that are collectible today are the tins with hinged tops, interesting shapes and decorative stencils or labels used by early companies no longer in existence. Many containers have pictures of scenes and buildings long since forgotten.

Tin containers were used for gunpowder, salve, shoe polish, tobacco, tea, coffee, cocoa, chocolate and many other products. They were of all sizes, from the large lunch pail to the tiniest embossed pillbox. In shape they were round, oval, square, oblong or fancy, including jewelry boxes with curved corners and *bombe* sides and dome tops made for Twin Oaks Tobacco.

Tin gunpowder cans are particularly interesting. Their shape is similar to a pocket flask, and they have a patent lead top. They were made in several sizes and usually had a paper label with a picture of Indians, hunters and dogs, quail or grouse, together with the name of the kind of powder and that of the manufacturer.

A gunpowder can marked GREEN MT. RIFLE POWDER, TIGER MILLS, BENNINGTON, has a label design of a man and a tiger. In 1845, the Bennington Powder Company marked its cans with a stencil with crossed rifles. Texas Rifle Powder was put up in Boston in a can with a picture of an Indian on the label, and Oriental Rifle Powder has a picture of a grouse on the can. The can labeled KENTUCKY RIFLE GUN POWDER, HAZZARD POWDER COMPANY has a man with rifle and dog in a woodland setting print that was engraved from a sketch by Catlin. The design is in a circle and the can is found in two sizes. "Orange Rifle Powder, Laflin and Hand Powder Company" was packed in a similar can, but the design shows a hunter sitting in a woodland setting with a dog beside him. The rarest of all gunpowder cans is the one with the label

ROGERS ORANGE GUN POWDER, NEW YORK. The circular label of the sportsman and dog is engraved by Rollinson. This gunpowder was also put up in kegs and pound papers, as well as tin canisters.

Tobacco was also packaged in cans, and such containers as the Tuxedo Tobacco, hip pocket shape, the red Forrest Stream Tobacco can, and Pioneer Brand, as well as the Lucky Strike tin, are all collectible. Old Abe Smoking Tobacco was manufactured by Gleidersdorf & Company and put up in paper packages and two-ounce tins with a picture of Abe Lincoln on both. Mayo's Tobacco and Patterson's Red Seal Tobacco came in tin lunch pails, and Schepps' Cocoanut was also packaged in a tin lunch pail with an embossed top. Mayo also packaged their cut-plug tobacco in a series of brownie tins of different designs. One can is in the form of a fat man with bald head, red coat, vest and elk's-tooth watch chain; he has a pipe in his mouth and holds a tin of Mayo's tobacco in his hand. These details are all painted on the can. Gillies Coffee was also put up in a tin lunch pail marked LUNCH PAIL COFFEE, but it was also in a tall tin marked EDWIN J. GILLIES & CO. HIGH GRADE COFFEE, N.Y.

Since many of the above brands no longer exist, or if they are still made are packaged differently, the old tins become historic and thus collectible. In 1871, Moore & Davies' Bogota Coffee was packaged in a tin, and Huyler's Cocoa, Baker's Chocolate and Rich's Canton Ginger were packaged in tins with attractive stencils or labels that date back to the last quarter of the nineteenth century. One Tetley Tea tin has a picture of an elephant. Another has the picture of the Boston Tea Party, and the Grand Union Tea Company at one time put up its tea in a can with a grinding machine attached.

Other nineteenth-century products packaged in tins of various sizes and shapes included Lee & Thorn Sons, Polish 1837, Patent French Polish, Pansy Brand Extract Soap Tree Bark, Temple Incense, California Nugget Chop Cut Tobacco, and Dr. Lyons Tooth Powder as early as 1875. There were many drugs packaged in flat, round embossed metal containers. Sulphate of quinine was in a square hinged box with a label showing women's fashions in the 1880's. An interesting tin box in the Landauer Collection at the New York Historical Society is a large, red tin book labeled: THE HEROLD BY B. M. SHIPMAN, N.Y. SOLE AGENT. This was probably used for shop-window advertisement rather than for packaging the book. Many of the tea, coffee, ginger and other spices were put up in gilded and decorated tin canisters, some of them made in China.

Spice boxes holding six small cans were bronzed and stenciled with the names of the spices. There were also tea and coffee canisters in various sizes and shapes. Large containers for spices were used in country stores in the mid-nineteenth century. These usually had bright, elaborately stenciled decorations. The large grocery store tins were made in this country by japanners who stenciled on them designs of Chinese figures, flowers and other patterns. Thomas Blakemore was a japanner in Philadelphia as early as 1823. In 1831, Henry and Thomas Francis of Philadelphia advertised: "Signs, trays, grocery store oil stands, tea canisters, with Chinese figures and other patterns." Daniel D. Dick of Philadelphia also japanned signs and grocers' canisters. In 1848, J. Hall Rohrman advertised in the Philadelphia *Direc-*

Cans with fancy shapes for tea, spices and other groceries. Late 19th century. COURTESY CAN MANUFACTURERS INSTITUTE.

Tetley tea cans through the years. COURTESY CAN MANUFACTURERS INSTITUTE.

tory: "Tea Chests, coffee bins, spice canisters, Oriental and Arabesque styles. Tea canisters, coffee canisters, spitoons, spice boxes, toy cups, match safes, jar covers, molasses cups, lanterns, sand boxes." However, it was some years later before this type of merchandise was made in great quantities.

In 1851, Tucker, Crofford & Rector, tinmakers of Albany, exhibited at the Crystal Palace: "Cans for powder, tea, coffee, spice, Round Japan Hyson, Oolong, showbowls, spice boxes." H. A. & E. A. Pelton of Albany also sold plain and japanned tinware. Other commercial suppliers of tin containers who also put out catalogues were C. H. & E. S. Goldberg of New York, George Fries & Company of Philadelphia (1859) and Benham and Stoutenborough of New York (1883). However, it is not possible to identify any of the cans with particular makers. Late dealers like John H. Locke & Company, New York City, advertised: "Stamped Japanned, Planished and Plain Tinware Goods—toys, watering cans, cake boxes, tea boxes and hip bottles." A trade card of Musgrove and Son, New York City, publicized: "Tin Goods for Wedding Presents—Emblematical of Different Trades and Professions." Tin cans and tin boxes were made by the Boston Can Company in 1886. In the late nineteenth century, Ginna & Company of New York also made tea and coffee canisters, spice cans and boxes for storing sugar, coffee, bay leaves and other grocery-store staples.

These many items of tin offer a fascinating field for the collector, even if he can only start with a tin cup or a child's alphabet plate made a few years ago. The eighteenth-century items are rare and expensive, but there are still some to be found. Later items are more available. The article itself gives a clue to the date—a tin plate warmer would be early, while tin nutmeg graters were made until a few years ago. The workmanship is the best indication of age and value, for the handmade article can usually be distinguished from the factory product.

II

Advertising Americana

New England painted inn sign. Early 19th century. COURTESY RHODE
ISLAND HISTORICAL SOCIETY.

American Glass Containers for Liquor, Medicine, etc.

THERE ARE an infinite number of free-blown and molded American bottles made as containers of medicine, snuff, liquor and other commercial products that are collectible today. These provide an interesting and comparatively inexpensive field for the collector. Such a collection not only offers variation in color, size and shape of bottle, but a little research will also reveal interesting data on the history of American industry and on early social customs. Many bottles have the impressed names of the glass companies that made them, and others have printed labels which establish the identity of the bottle's contents with the company that made it and thus constitute a page in the history of American advertising.

It was the demand for bottles as containers for liquor, medicine and other household products that made the manufacture of common bottles and containers either a principal product or a sideline with practically all of the Early American glasshouses. This connection between glassmaking and trade also goes back to the earliest European-made wine or spirit bottles of the seventeenth century. These early wine bottles were crude. They were blown from dark olive-green or dark olive-amber glass known as black glass.

The earliest bottles had a long neck with a thin ring about one half inch below the lip and a bulbous body. Later wine bottles continued to have a bulbous body, but the neck gradually became shorter until the middle of the eighteenth century when the form evolved to a slender, more cylindrical shape with a cylindrical neck. By 1800, the tall cylindrical body with high, rounded shoulders and wide, sloping collared lip appeared. The later bottles were molded. Although there is proof in the old ads that such wine bottles were made in American glasshouses and we can determine the dates of bottles by their shape, it is impossible to distinguish the American from the imported bottles. Most of the old excavated wine bottles which were used in trading with the Indians were of foreign manufacture. Several initialed wine bottles—the only such identified as American—were made at the Mt. Vernon Glass Company in New York State between 1810 and 1820. They are deep green, and although quite rare today, must have been made and initialed to order in considerable quantity. One type of free-blown wine bottle of bulbous shape with a long, tapering cylindrical neck is called a Hogarth bottle in England. Some of similar shape were made at Ludlow, Massachusetts, around 1815 and are known as Ludlow bottles. This type was probably made much earlier by Wistar and Stiegel. They range in size from $3\frac{1}{8}''$ to $11\frac{1}{2}''$ in height. Carboys were used for shipping liquor, and usually had a wicker covering which in early times was woven by the Indians. Carboys were made from Revolutionary times until 1840. They range in color from amber, olive amber, dark brown amber to dark olive green.

Carboys were made in Keene, New Hampshire, in New York, Connecticut, and even in Ohio.

Another type of old liquor bottle is the tall, tapering four-sided, square-case bottle generally used for rum or gin. These were called case bottles because they were packed by dozens in a wooden box or case. They were blown from dark olive-green or olive-amber bottle glass and ranged in size from one and one half to two quarts. Rare old gin bottles have a seal and the owner's initials.

Besides wine and spirit bottles, American glasshouses made a great variety of other free-blown bottles from earliest times down through the middle and end of the nineteenth century, as is revealed in the following ads. As early as 1754, Thomas Lepper of New York advertised: "All sorts of Bottles from 1 Quart to 3 Gallons and upwards * * * all Gentlemen that want Bottles of any size with their names on them or any Chymical glasses or other sort of Glass Ware by applying to said Lepper have them made with all Expedition." Wistar and Stiegel also made all sorts of ordinary bottles including snuff, mustard and "junk" bottles. By the beginning of the nineteenth century, many commercial glass works were established to make trade bottles.

In 1819, O'Hara & Craigg at the Pittsburgh Glass Works advertised: "Bottles of all Kinds of any quantity, together with pocket flasks, pickling jars, apothecarys shop furniture or other hollowware." But of all the advertisements those of the Kensington Glass Works in Philadelphia give us the most information about the glass made in America in the early nineteenth century.

In 1824, Dr. Dyott advertised the products of his Phila-delphia and Kensington Glass Works. Since Dyott advertised

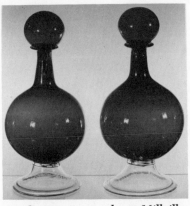

Apothecary jars made at Millville, N.J., 1836, for Dr. Schley's Drug Store. Sapphire blue with clear-glass base. COURTESY NEW YORK HISTORICAL SOCIETY.

Cod-liver oil bottle, amber glass. American, 19th century. COURTESY NEW YORK HISTORICAL SOCIETY.

Amber coachman bottle marked: "Van Duncks, Genever, Ware & Schmitz." Whiskey bottle, 1850. COURTESY NEW YORK HISTORICAL SOCIETY.

Cologne bottle of clear glass with leaf decoration. American, 19th century. COURTESY NEW YORK HISTORICAL SOCIETY.

throughout the United States, he must have at one time furnished an overwhelming majority of the common bottles in use. The ad lists many varieties of bottles including:

Apothecaries Vials from Drachm to eight ounces
Patent Medicine Vials of every description
Tincture bottles with ground stoppers from ½ pt. to 1 gal.
Specie bottles with lacquered covers, ½ pt. to 2 gal.
Druggist packing bottles, wide & narrow mouths, ½ pt. to 2 gal.
Acid bottles with ground stoppers
Carboys
Demijohns from one quart to two gallons
Confectioners show bottles and preserving do.
Pickling & preserving Jars, straight & turned over tops, from ½ pt. to 1 gal.
Quart and half gallon bottles
Washington, LaFayette, Franklin, Ship Franklin, Agriculture and Masonic Cornucopia, American Eagle & common ribbed Pocket Flasks
Seltzer water, mustard & Cayenne pepper bottles
Snuff, blacking and ink bottles
with every other description of vials and bottles made to order.

Snuff bottles blown in light amber, olive amber and greenish amber were made at the Coventry Glassworks in Connecticut from 1813 to 1842, as well as many other contemporary glassworks. Snuff bottles are usually one half pound or larger and are of plain blown glass with space for a paper label. Similar snuff bottles have labels of Lorillard, Hamilton, and Maccoboy snuff. A molded snuff bottle has the inscription: E. ROOME, TROY, NEW YORK and was made in the 1840's. Preserve and fruit bottles are large and have wide, open necks. A typical pickle bottle holds two quarts and is tall and rectangular in shape with a collared neck and an impressed design of Gothic tracery. It is usually found in aquamarine.

Ink bottles were made in dark amber, aquamarine and olive green. They were usually funnel shaped with a circular base and a short neck. An unusual ribbed ink bottle with a pen rest is marked HOOKERS INK. At Glassboro, ink bottles were listed: "Durable, plain, old, pyramid, and oval."

In 1830, the Franklin and the Harmony Glass companies of New Jersey advertised: "Vials, quart and packing bottles, castor oil bottles, flasks, jars." By 1848, there were seven glassworks listed in the Philadelphia directory, all making vials, carboys and patent-medicine bottles. They were Dyott-ville Glass Works; Whitney & Brother; Union Glass Works; Kensington Bottle and Glass Works; Phoenix Glass Works; Eagle Glass Works; and Burgin & Pearsall.

The Eagle Glass Works advertised blue, red, and green cologne bottles, in addition to druggist vials, ink bottles and mineral-water bottles. Between 1825 and 1844, the Mt. Vernon Glass Company of New York State made chestnut bottles, vials and other blown bottles, as well as historical flasks. The principal products at Saratoga Glass Works at about this time were also snuff, medicine, spring-water bottles and historical flasks. The figure of Moses striking the rock advertised Poland Water. The Peterboro Glass Works and the Lockport Glass Works also made free-blown bottles and jars, and in 1879, the Ellenville Glass Factory manufactured bottles, carboys, fruit jars and demijohns. In 1846, P. C. Dummer & Company advertised: "Druggists' flint and green glass chemi-

Top row, left to right: Soda bottles; pale aquamarine free-blown medicine bottles; three bitters bottles; utility bottles.

Center row, left to right: Gothic-design bottles for pickles, capers and pepper sauce; ink bottle; opaque blue-paneled perfume bottle, sapphire-blue blown and molded perfume bottle, molded lion cologne bottle, molded wicker-design bottle, Gothic perfume bottle, two rare amethyst and blue-green paneled cologne bottles; utility bottle; bottle marked: "LaFayette's," with molded profile of Lafayette.

Bottom row, left to right: Pitkin flask, square-necked gin bottle, porter or beer bottle, black glass; cologne bottle with molded design; three hand-blown bottles with swirled ribbing, flask, pattern-molded; free-blown nursing bottle, black glass free-blown wine bottle, amber "Ludlow" bottle.

cal furniture, fancy bottles, and vials of all descriptions. Private moulds and bottles made to order."

From 1848 to 1852, a Glassboro, New Jersey, glasshouse was making demijohns of gallon size, pickle jars, jelly jars, vials, inkwells, cologne bottles and patent-medicine bottles with the name of the medicine and the dispenser put in the mold. Well-known bottles made at Stangers Glassboro Works were Townsend's Sarsaparilla, Keeler's, Panacea, Turkish Balsam, Hart's Extract, Harlem Oil, Cherokee Liniment, Turlington Balsam, Kelly's Ovals, Opodoldoc, Hohnstock's Vermifuge, Paul's Russian Oil, Morse's Syrup, Hunt's Liniment, Blake's Bitters, and Flander's Grecian Drops. Cologne bottles were also made and were designated by pattern such as tree, dahlia, grape, fountain, lion and diamond. In the 1860's and 1870's, the Harmony Glass Works of South Jersey made many flasks and also the well-known Booz bottle and many other containers for bitters. In 1866, the Brooklyn Green Glass Works was supplying druggists, perfumers, confectioners and liquor dealers with glass. They also painted apothecary labels and furnished such stores for business. Excelsior Flint Glass Works of New York manufactured flint and green glass for druggists, perfumers, confectioners and liquor dealers.

In 1868, such bottles were manufactured in Philadelphia by F. & J. Bodine; Whitney Glass Works; B. H. Sleeper & Company; and Dyottville Glass Works. In the 1880's, Whitehall, Tatum & Company was one of the largest glass manufacturers. At about this same date the Lancaster Glass Works also made bitters bottles and other medicine bottles. The ads of the New Granite Glass Works also included: "Private Moulds," and "Demijohns, Flasks, Wine, Soda, Mineral Ale,

Ink, Blacking, Bay Water Cologne, Hair Oil, Patent Medicine and all other kinds of Bottles, etc. Black, Green and
Amber Ware." Early two-piece Moxie bottles of blue aquamarine with straight sides and the inscription MOXIE NERVE
FOOD, LOWELL, MASS. PATENTED were made at the Lyndeboro
Glass Company. Bottles and demijohns and physicians' and
apothecaries' equipment were also made at all Midwestern
glasshouses.

The early medicine vials and bottles were blown from
ordinary bottle glass and were in shades of amber, olive
amber, olive green and aquamarine. They were blown in
many different sizes and shapes, from the long, rectangular
vial with short neck to the tiny bulbous-base, long-neck,
lipped type. Patent medicines were put up in bottles made
in piece molds or in private molds, with the name of the
medicine and the dispenser. One such bottle reads: DR.
ROBERTSON'S FAMILY MEDICINE PREPARED ONLY BY T. W. DYOTT.
These patent-medicine bottles were rectangular in form and
range from about 4" to 6" in height. The early ones were
usually made in shades of green, while later medicine bottles
are of clear glass. Plain bottles are sometimes found with
printed labels.

Early snuff and shoe-blacking bottles were usually free
blown from amber, green, or olive-amber or olive-green bottle glass. Shoe-blacking bottles are usually rectangular with
long, straight sides. Dispensers seldom owned their own
molds, instead they purchased plain bottles and put on their
own printed labels. Thus, although such bottles vary in size
and shape, the same type bottle is often found with the label
of two different dispensers.

In 1839, James S. Mason advertised Challenge Blacking

"Put up in 1, 2, 3, 4, 5, 6, 8, and 12 oz. bottles." If a bottle is found with an original label this helps in dating it. Bottles with the label of A. Bostwick, blacking and ink manufacturer of Albany, were made in 1832 or 1833. Shoe-blacking bottles are usually around five inches tall and are more often darker shades of olive or amber green. Occasionally a shoe-blacking bottle is blown in a mold and may have the name of the maker cut into the mold.

Druggist and confectioners show bottles were of several types. Tall, straight-sided pint or quart bottles with short necks were used to store chemicals, candies and other products on the shelves. A druggist might have rows of these clear-white bottles marked with gold-and-black hand-painted labels. Some were made of opaque white glass. Those of pottery with elaborately decorated labels were usually from France or England. The tall, vase-shaped fancy-stopper containers for apothecaries' window were made of clear glass and were usually filled with colored liquid.

Confectioners' bottles were of various shapes. There were plain tin-covered jars and squatty wide jars with heavy pressed-glass covers, and similar jars of quart size. Tall, vase-shaped jars with similar covers or heavy covers with knobs were used for window display. Later these bottles were cut and engraved. Many are still to be seen on display in stores. They date from the 1870's and 1880's, although according to their ads some were made by the Kensington Glass Works as early as 1825.

There are certain characteristics to look for in bottle collecting. Free-blown bottles can be identified by their irregular shapes, and no two free-blown bottles are exactly alike. These bottles are expensive and not common, since few utility bottles were free blown after 1860. The free-blown bottle with a pontil mark on its base is usually old and valuable. Bottles blown in the mold in the first part of the nineteenth century had the neck and lip finished by hand. Later the complete bottle was made in the mold. Old bottles made before the invention of the automatic bottlemaking machinery have applied lips. In the machine-made bottle the lip is made in the mold so that the mold seam also runs through the lip. Most American medicine bottles were made in two piece molds and can be identified by the mold seams on the bottles. Bottles with embossed lettering are valuable in relation to the content of the lettering. Bottles embossed with a glassmaker's name such as Dyott, Lancaster or Saratoga are sought after, and bottles with the names of medicines and liquor no longer made are collectible. Bitters bottles will soon be in as much demand as historical flasks.

Bottles are also collected for shape and color. Brilliant and rare colors are popular, and any figure or whimsy bottle is collectible regardless of its age. Bitters bottles and flasks have been well documented and are now an important and expensive field of collecting. There are detailed books on the subject.

Trade Paperweights

O F ALL the gadgets contrived for the purpose of advertising goods, one of the cleverest and most successful was the paperweight. The paperweight is not only convenient for the office desk but is also useful in the home. For this reason these paperweights were not readily consigned to the ash barrel and there are many of them to be found today.

Paperweights were made in France as early as 1820, but it was 1850 before they were made in any quantity in America, and certainly the 1870's before they were employed as an advertising medium. In 1876, paperweights were made with the Philadelphia Centennial buildings as subject matter. The designs were pressed in the glass from the back and the lettering was done in gold leaf or lustrous paint. A weight of this type was made with an impressed likeness of Queen Victoria painted in blue. It advertised the Victoria Hotel in Chicago. The U.S. Glass Company, Pittsburgh, Pennsylvania, made a paperweight with the head of a girl and the firm's name impressed in clear glass. In about 1885, pictures on porcelain were encased in glass paperweights, and plaster figures called sulphites were also encased in glass. From about 1880 until World War I, paperweights with names of companies or products were given away as souvenirs by many companies which found they created good business.

The first advertising weights had the lettering and design made entirely of glass in candy-cane blue-and-red patterns or simple black-and-white lettering in glass. The following paperweights in the Bella C. Landauer Collection at the New York Historical Society are of this type: S. P. Skinner & Company—Clear glass weight with green-glass center and lettering in red glass; M. Seypana & Company, Wholesale Bakers—Clear-glass weight with lettering in candy-cane blue-and-red glass; T. Thornley, Sign Painter, Trenton, New Jersey—Black-and-white lettering; American Fire—Philadelphia Eagle and lettering in black and white; K.G.E.—Eagle & Shield, "Fidelity, Valor, Honor," in colored glass. Other weights have embossed or impressed lettering in clear or frosted glass upon the surface of the paperweight.

Undoubtedly many glass companies made these advertising paperweights, but those we know about definitely are the Libby Glass Company, which in 1893 made paperweights with pictures of the World's Columbian Exposition buildings in color; the New York Glass Company, which made paperweights for the American Fire Insurance Company, Philadelphia, with the design of an eagle in white-and-clear glass; the U.S. Glass Company of Pittsburgh, which made paperweights with a head of frosted glass impressed and a dot border with the firm name raised on the surface. In 1891, this company advertised: "Clear-glass paperweights." The Spring City Glass Works of Philadelphia made a weight with a shield and star and its name in frosted glass, and an unidentified glass company made a paperweight with the following inscription: A POINTER—THE LOOKING GLASS PAPER-

American advertising paperweights. Lithographs under glass, 20th century. COURTESY NEW YORK HISTORICAL SOCIETY, BELLA C. LANDAUER COLLECTION.

WEIGHT FOR EFFECTIVE PERMANENT, AND VISIBLE ADVERTISING. The Kristol Flint Glass Company made clear weights with a stemmed cut-glass bowl. All of these are now rare.

Many paperweights had small objects sealed in the glass, such as the weight of M. M. Rhodes & Son, Taunton, Massachusetts, which enclosed shoe buttons. Pins or rocks or metals may be enclosed in the glass, as in the early Prudential Life Insurance Company's weight which has a chip of the Rock of Gibralter.

Trademarks, pictures of buildings, pictures of the product to be sold and portraits are all found on the printed papers pasted under the glass dome of the nineteenth-century advertising paperweight. There were pictures of scenery such as Niagara Falls, Plymouth Rock, Yellowstone Park, Grant's Tomb, Barnum's Circus Monument at Seaside Park, New Jersey, the buildings of the Columbian Exposition in 1893, the Louisiana Purchase Exposition and the White House. Buildings also include many shop fronts and factory buildings which are no longer in existence but which may have historical interest. The portraits and signatures of owners of a shop or factory often include those of well-known industrialists. There are also pictures of historical and patriotic personalities such as Lincoln, Grant, Admiral Dewey, President McKinley, Henry Hudson and President Taft.

Flowers, animals and colored sentimental pictures are also found on paperweights used to advertise products. But the most sought after weights are those with pictures of old fire engines, locomotives, stagecoaches, surreys, sulkies or delivery wagons. There are paperweights with pictures of old sewing machines, early pianos, old-fashioned shoes, spinning wheels and the printing press, as shown in the weight advertising

Babcock Printing Press Manufacturing, New London, Connecticut. There are also paperweights showing pianos and organs, such as the colored scene of women at the organ which was distributed by the Estey Organ Company of Brattleboro, Massachusetts; and the weight with a picture of the Gold Medal Pianoforte. Old-type wagons are pictured on paperweights of the Auburn Wagon Company, Greencastle, Pennsylvania; the Hecker Jones Milling Company; the Henry Hooker Carriage Company; and the Buffalo Spring and Gear Company.

You will find commercial paperweights in most antique and secondhand shops today. They range in price from 50¢ to $10, depending on their subject matter and condition. Those with candy-cane decoration or designs impressed in the glass or raised borders of glass are more valuable than those with a picture glued underneath the glass dome. Paperweights with pictures are more often rectangular than round in shape. Paperweights with chips or nicks in the glass have little value.

In addition to glass paperweights, there were many advertising paperweights made of various metals, as well as of marble and other materials. These are usually interesting in shape, since they include forms of animals, men, shoes, books, barrels and other objects in three dimensions. They are made of iron, bronze, brass, copper, aluminum, marble, plastic and other materials. There is the pig-iron paperweight advertising pig iron by C. W. Stetson & Company and also by H. W. Adams & Company; the bronze cow awarded for exceptional service in the Prina Mills, St. Louis, Missouri; the iron bulldog advertising "segars"; the iron elephant of the Crane Company's anniversary 1855–1905; the iron fat man advertising Thatcher Boiler and Furnaces. Owls are on a paperweight of the Deoxidized Manufacturing Company of Bridgeport, Connecticut.

The National Security Company put out a metal paperweight with an eagle atop a globe of the world, and an eagle on piers is on the Krabuter Company, Newark, New Jersey. The Salamander Company had a paperweight with a large metal fly. Blue-fields Bananas distributed one with a bunch of brass bananas on an iron base. An iron buffalo with the inscription PAN AMERICAN 1901 is an interesting weight, and the bust of Shakespeare marked JAS. B. REGAN IMPORT CO., NEW YORK CIGARS is also unique. A brass Yale key in a lock rests on a black metal base; a General Electric radio tube is set on a brass base; and an aluminum model of an oil burner advertises Oil-O-Matic. Wm. Skinner & Company, silk mills, put out a paperweight with a design of a metal Indian on its seventy-fifth anniversary in 1923. There are also weights in the form of white or black marble books, marble cubes and obelisks and pyramids of iron.

Perhaps some of the figures on metal weights were modeled by well-known sculptors, but there is no record of this and so they must be collected solely for the variety of their shapes and for the names of the companies that used them as a means of goodwill through advertising. There are several hundred of these advertising paperweights in the Bella C. Landauer Collection. Many private collectors have equally large numbers, and similar paperweights are to be found at reasonable prices in secondhand stores, junk shops and antique shops. All in all there are thousands of them and no one collector can hope to own an example of every one.

Their value depends upon the subject matter and the

*American, 19th-century iron and bronze
advertising paperweights.* COURTESY NEW
YORK HISTORICAL SOCIETY, BELLA C.
LANDAUER COLLECTION.

condition of the glass. They are objects of business and social history and have no aesthetic value. However, a collection of advertising paperweights will be of considerable monetary value someday. Closely related to the metal paperweight are the metal clips, novelty advertising banks and metal inkwells which are all to be found marked with the names of shops and manufacturers.

Advertising Fans and Fancy Cardboard Souvenirs

IN EUROPE in the eighteenth century, paper fans were hand painted with scenes of famous places and events such as bull fights, operas, historical buildings and other social and historical scenes and places. These were folding paper fans. Those of this type in the Metropolitan Museum of Art include one with a scene of Rossini's *Barber of Seville,* one with a medallion scene of the Roman Coliseum, one with the London Crystal Palace, and one with early battle scenes and the Rock of Gibraltar. These fans are all hand painted and have beautiful borders. The museum also owns the original sketches for an eighteenth-century fan with a scene of Vesuvius in eruption, and for one with scenes of the Paris Exposition in 1889, and one of T. A. Steinman's lithographed French fans with advertising of the nineteenth century.

Hand-painted fans were not made in America, with the exception of a few which were hand painted to order with scenes of country estates or portraits. Although there are two notices of early fan painting in America, these were probably painted on silk. In 1774, John and Hamilton Stevenson advertised: "Painting on silk, sattin, etc. Fan Painting," in the South Carolina and American *General Gazette,* and in the

Pennsylvania Journal in 1782, John Walters, miniature painter, advertised: "Coat of Arms and fans painted."

The earliest American fans made in any quantity were probably those lithographed with a scene of the New York Crystal Palace of 1853 as the center of decoration. There is a collection of lithographed fans with scenes of Concord, Massachusetts, in the Concord Antiquarian Society. These include the Old North Bridge, Meriam's Corner, Ralph Waldo Emerson, Orchard House—the home of the Alcott's— Old Manse—Nathaniel Hawthorne's home—and the Minute Men. These fans were made as souvenirs of a visit to Concord.

In 1876, a folding fan with a large picture of the Centennial Buildings in Philadelphia printed in black on a cream ground was made for sale at the Exposition. One of these fans of historical value is in the Bella C. Landauer Collection. A lithographed folding fan used as an advertisement for Wanamaker's Philadelphia store was also made at about this date. It has three sepia scenes of the store, two interior and one exterior, set in medallions surrounded by floral decorations in green and white.

A souvenir fan of the Café Martin, New York, shows a street scene of New York and the sidewalk café in the late nineteenth century, before the day of the automobile. The Café Martin also gave away a similar fan picturing a man and girl in an automobile. The Knickerbocker Restaurant distributed as many as four different souvenir fans with French scenes and girls. The most interesting of these shows a scene with an early touring car driving through a flock of geese. A folding fan with a masque decorated in black and gold advertised the Central Park Casino. Many of these fans were at first made in France, but later they were made in

Centennial fan, Philadelphia, 1876. Black print on cream ground.
COURTESY NEW YORK HISTORICAL SOCIETY, BELLA C. LANDAUER
COLLECTION.

Souvenir fan, World's Columbian Exposition, Chicago, Ill., 1892.
COURTESY NEW YORK HISTORICAL SOCIETY.

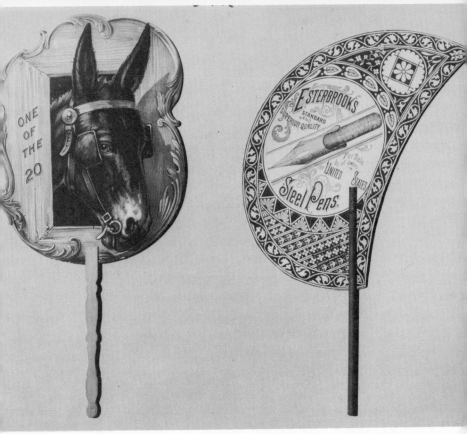

American advertising fans. COURTESY NEW YORK HISTORICAL SOCIETY, BELLA C. LANDAUER COLLECTION.

American advertising fans, 20th century. COURTESY NEW YORK HISTORICAL SOCIETY, BELLA C. LANDAUER COLLECTION.

Japan, and often had Japanese scenes with figures and flowers. Folding fans advertised the Ziegfield Midnight Frolic, Ross Wier & Company, Coffee; Tip-Top Bread; Bissells' Carpet Sweeper; and such well-known hotels as the old Waldorf-Astoria, the Pennsylvania and the Hotel Martinique. One fan of the Knickerbocker Hotel has pictures of early airplanes. The Hotel Lafayette fan has a Japanese scene. Some have tiny mirrors and others rules of etiquette printed on them. Fragrant Vanity Fair cigarettes and many other products were advertised on these early fans. Around 1900, Bloomingdale's gave away a folding blue tissue-paper fan set on a metal handle.

However, fan advertising was generally done by means of cheaper flat cardboard fans with a scene on the front and advertising on the back, although many firms used both sides for advertising. In an amusing cartoon in *Judge* in 1886, the advertising business and its souvenirs are caricatured, and in the corner of the picture hangs a group of advertising fans. When the Manhattan Market opened on June 8, 1880, fans with a picture of the market were given away. In 1883, William Hills & Company, Broadway, New York, gave away fans with snow scenes, autumn scenes and girls' heads in a daisy. T. K. Horton of Brooklyn had fans printed with scenes of girls playing guitars and mandolins. In 1887, the Great Atlantic and Pacific Company put out a series of advertising fans with the following titles, so characteristic of the age: "Pet of the Yacht" (boys) ; "Pride of the Yacht" (girl); "Grandmother's Pet"; "Gilbert & Sullivan's, 3 Maids from Mikado"; "Dress Parade" (child and dog); "Over the Garden Wall" (mother and children); "Grandmother in the Row Boat"; "Shady Nook by the River"; "Girls at the Sea Shore."

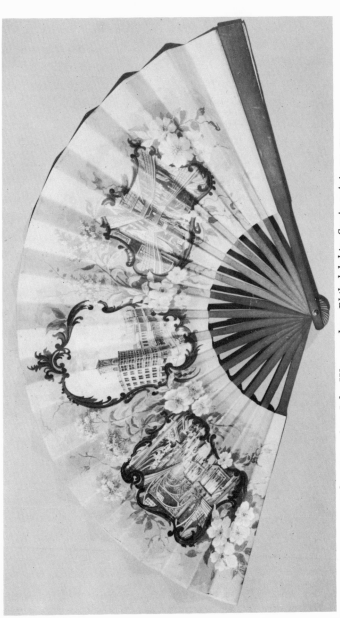

Advertising fan, John Wanamaker, Philadelphia. Sepia prints on green ground. COURTESY NEW YORK HISTORICAL SOCIETY, BELLA C. LANDAUER COLLECTION.

The Siegal Cooper Company distributed an advertising fan which read: "Meet me at the Fountain, The Coolest Spot in New York." Esterbrook's Steel Pens were advertised on a crescent-shaped cardboard fan. Raffer's Coffee, 20 Mule Team Borax and many other well-known products were also advertised on cardboard fans. The scenes usually included pictures of children, pretty girls, snow scenes, autumn or patriotic scenes, but often a picture of the store or product advertised was included. During presidential campaigns fans with pictures of the candidates were popular. The fan made for the Dudley Shoe Company, Newport, New Hampshire, has a picture of Washington, Lincoln and Woodrow Wilson. Bird's Business Institute distributed a fan with a picture of a Gibson girl.

Fans were also made in the shape of lanterns and artists' easels. One in the shape of a purse has a picture of Lillian Russell. The Siegal Cooper Company gave away a fan with a picture of its store, and in 1902, the R. H. Macy Company distributed a fan with a picture of its store. Early in its history, Lord & Taylor used advertising fans with pictures of various breeds of dogs, one with a Negro baby, and one with a woman and child under an umbrella. The Eagle Condensed Milk Company advertising fans had a picture of a child and dog, and Borden's had one with a picture of a butterfly and girl. Sailors and Boston Harbor in 1773 were shown on the fan that advertised Magic Yeast.

In addition to cardboard advertising fans, there were palm leaf fans printed with names of companies and their products, and there were also bamboo fans covered with thin Japanese paper on which were printed Oriental scenes together with the name of a company and product. Of course the use of advertising fans has not been altogether discontinued, although they are not nearly as popular as they were in the 1880's and early 1900's. But there are still fans that say "Dewey," "Win with Taft," "Truman for Congress" and "I'm a Douglas Fan." There is one advertising "S. Klein on the Square," the Starlight Roof of the Waldorf, the *Journal American* and the Greenwich Savings Bank. They may be of little value today, but the time will come when a collection of advertising fans will be of historical as well as social value. The time has already arrived when the accumulator has taken his place along with the collector as a preserver of social history and advertising Americana.

Closely related to advertising fans are the fancy cardboard souvenirs with advertisements printed on the back. These were made in various shapes and were printed in gaudy colors with sentimental subjects including children, pets, pretty women and flowers. Part of the picture was often embossed. It is seldom possible to know the exact date of these souvenirs, but they are all of the vintage of the late nineteenth and early twentieth centuries.

The most interesting feature of most of them was their fancy shape, and many were indeed unique. The W. Frear Dry Goods Store of Troy, New York, had colorful cardboard souvenirs in the shape of shoes, a dustpan, a whisk broom and a bellows. Heathers store in New York had a series of colorful cardboard souvenirs with cats and dogs in baskets. Other stores had their names printed on baskets filled with flowers. There is a unique lady in a hammock, a girl in a swing, a George Washington hatchet and a bird cage.

Other cardboard souvenirs are in the shape of birds, dolls, butterflies, shells or a Puss in Boots. Still other stores gave

COLLECTING SMALL ANTIQUES

away cardboard souvenirs in the shape of Santa Claus or a
Christmas tree or a grandfather's clock. Aunt Jemina's Pan-
cake Flour advertised its product with a cardboard mask for
the face. Chase & Sanborn advertised on a fancy cardboard
cup. A teacup was also used by Atlantic & Pacific, and a teapot by Wilder & Rice, Windsor, Vermont. Friends' Oats used
a cutout child in costume, and Gold Label Flour had a fancy
cardboard souvenir in the shape of a rabbit. A sled, a wheelbarrow, a pug dog on a cushion, a baby in a cradle, children
in a balloon and a Greek statue were some of the other shapes
used. Huyler's advertised on a hog shape at one time, and
again, probably at Easter, its advertisement was in the form
of a cross. An Easter egg was used by the Jas. Van Dyk Tea
Company, New York, and Easter rabbits were also used.
Heinz advertised with a cutout cardboard pickle.

Small fans, artists' palettes and butterflies were used in
great numbers by many different companies. At one time
Magic Yeast gave away a cardboard saw that read: "Greatest
Bargain I Ever Saw," and an owl on which was printed,
"It's Owl Right." A large cardboard bucket has the printed
verses of the song, "The Old Oaken Bucket" and the name
of Dey Bros. & Company, Elmira & Syracuse, New York.

Other cardboard souvenirs with printed advertisements
include small trays and saucers to be used as pin trays. All
these colorful relics of the past are collectible today. They
are found in old trunks, old scrapbooks and for sale at secondhand shops and at antique shows. We can hardly call them
antiques, yet they are as old as many other articles now passed
as antiques, and since they are no longer used they become
curiosities and even rarities. Again I say, "If the museums
collect them, why not you or I?"

Watch Papers

WATCH PAPERS long neglected by collectors are now becoming popular. Many museums have collections and there are a few comprehensive private collections. Watch papers were originally used as a packing between the inner and outer case of a watch, to protect the works. From the mid-eighteenth century they became keepsakes. Women embroidered flower patterns on silk watch papers and make cutout or pinpricked designs of hearts, doves, forget-me-nots and wreaths. These keepsake watch papers were also made of woven hair or were crocheted from fine silk thread or quilted. Hand-stitched monograms in wreaths of laurel or moss roses and hand-painted watch papers are especially attractive. Early handmade watch papers were often in the form of a valentine or birthday greeting or in memory of the dead, showing a tombstone shadowed by a weeping willow. Examples have also been found with the Lord's Prayer in minute handwriting and with a miniature map of part of the United States.

But the watch papers which the collector of advertising Americana is interested in are the engraved papers used as an advertising medium by the watchmaker. In addition to this, the labels themselves are usually attractive, and many of them were engraved by well-known American artists, so that they may have real esthetic value.

By the beginning of the nineteenth century, watchmakers realized that these small, round papers in the back of a watch could be put to a useful purpose as an advertising medium. It soon became the custom, when a watch was cleaned or repaired, for the watchmaker to insert his own paper, showing an engraved scene with his name and the location of his shop. On the reverse of the paper he might note the price and date of repairs.

Watch papers are not found in every old watch, for the tiny papers are easily destroyed, but there are many watches stored away in collections and safe-deposit boxes that contain old engraved papers, and many watches contain not only one paper but several. In my recent search for old watch papers the curator of the Morgan collection of watches in the Metropolitan Museum opened up many of the watches in the collection and one watch was found to contain eight papers.

The first notice of an American watch paper was in the ad of a New York printer, Hugh Gaine, in 1758. In the Boston *Gazette* in 1758, a notice of a lost watch refers to the watch papers: "Moses Peck on the paper in the case." In the same year, Hugh Gaine advertised in the New York *Mercury* on December 4, 1758: "A beautiful Print in Miniature, of that truly Great Patriot, The Honorable Mr. Secretary Pitt, Adapted for watches." Portraits of other celebrities engraved by Nathaniel Hurd were advertised in the Boston *Evening Post,* December 27, 1762: "Engraved likenesses of King George the Third, William Pitt, and General Wolfe which could serve as watch papers." In 1768, Mervin Perry, watchmaker of New York, advertised: "Neat watch papers," and

American 19th-century watch papers, including rare Simon Willard. COURTESY CLOCKMAKER MUSEUM OF MR. BARNY. PHOTO BY MR. BARNY.

American watch paper. P. Maverick, Engraver. COURTESY NEW YORK HISTORICAL SOCIETY.

in the *Constitutional Gazette,* May 11, 1776, there appeared the following notice: "Lost . . . a silver watch with a china face, steel chain, the swivel has been newly brazed in and goes stiff, has been lately cleaned by White Matlock of this city and has one of his papers in the case."

In the category of watch papers, the collector may gather them because of the watchmaker's name or he may be concerned only with the design of the watch paper and the artist who engraved it. While every engraved watch paper has the name of the watchmaker or watch repairman, the beauty of the designs varies. There are comparatively few marked with an engraver's name. Although the designs differ, there are certain subjects such as hourglasses, Father Time, watches, eagles, Justice, ships, anchors and draped figures and cherubs that were the most popular. In the *Pennsylvania Packet,* September 16, 1779, John Walters of Philadelphia advertised: "General Washington's head in a watch paper, coloured or plain." Thomas Coram of Charleston, South Carolina, advertised in the *South Carolina and American General Gazette,* July 20, 1779, that he had completed an engraving of the engagement at Sullivan's Island and had printed it on a "watch case print . . . also on white satin." As far as we know, these particular rare watch papers are not known today, but they may well be in existence. A portrait of Washington being crowned by a cherub and a maiden is on the paper of E. D. Fowler, Fair Haven, Connecticut, copies of which have been found.

A line engraving of an hourglass, eagle's wings, a beehive and flowers is signed "Rollinson" and was made for J. Catlin, clock and watchmaker, Augusta, Georgia, in about 1830. The Rollinson watch papers in the James Arthur collection of clocks and watches at New York University were made for A. Henderson, watchmaker of Poughkeepsie. There are three papers, one engraved on yellow, one on pale blue, and a third on light rose. Each seems to have been made on a different plate although the design is the same. Above an oval with the inscription, "A. Henderson, Pokeepsie, clocks and watches of every description repaired and warranted," is an eagle with spread wings, and on either side of the inscription are robed figures—Justice with scales and a sword, and one with a rope and anchor. The figures stand on a strip of land surrounded by water.

Another interesting watch-paper design shows maidens under a canopy supporting the card of Church and Rogers, Watch Makers, Hartford, Connecticut. The design is by the well-known engraver Abner Reed. The watch paper of H. Ducommun, Philadelphia, has a design of Aurora's car with the wheels made like a watch face. A similar design bears the name of Wm. Middifield, clock and watchmaker, Fayetteville, North Carolina. The interesting design of two women in front of a watchmaker's window was also used by several different makers. The design in the American Antiquarian Society has the name of T. Russell, Watch Maker, Woodstock, Vermont. A similar design in the Metropolitan Museum is marked, "Roberts, Watchmaker, Trenton, N. J.," and in the Print Department of the Metropolitan is a similar design which also includes a Masonic emblem and has the signature, "A. Reed, *fecit*." It has the name of Judah Hart, Watchmaker, Norwich, Connecticut.

Also in the Metropolitan is a watch paper with a design of a wreath of leaves and flowers and a blank center by J. W. Orr. Indeed the same design is often found with the names of different watchmakers; the watchmaker could buy the design with a blank center and have his name added. Many watch papers have attractive decorative borders of lines, circles, leaves and other conventional patterns. Watch papers also often have inscriptions of directions for winding. The paper of Frederick Oakes, which is in the Metropolitan Museum, has a design of an eagle holding up a sign that reads, "Move the regulator with the sun to make the watch go faster—against the sun to go slower." Another watch paper has this direction in the border: "To make the watch go slower turn the regulator the same way you would wind up."

A watch paper from Frenchtown, New Jersey, in 1880, read: "Wind with care and use me well and let me have fair play. And I to U will try to tell the precise time of day. If I should chance to stop or fail to give the hour, take me to Miller's Shop, Frenchtown, N. J. and he will give me power." The words were arranged in verse form to make a decoration for the paper.

Watch papers were both printed and engraved on white, cream, buff, orange, blue, green, yellow or rose paper. Sometimes they were printed in combinations of colors such as white on silver, gold on blue, blue on gold or red or green on white. Watch papers vary in size from 1½″ to 2½″ in diameter, but the common size seems to be about 2″ in diameter. Watch papers also vary in thickness, and the earliest ones are on thicker and better-grade paper.

A check list of watch papers would give the names of the majority of watch- and clockmakers of America in the eighteenth and nineteenth centuries. However, the concern of this chapter is not with the names of watchmakers but with the watch papers themselves, and since the value of a watch paper—with the exception of those which bear the names of such famous makers as Aaron Willard or Simon Willard, Jun.—is primarily in the engraving itself and in the engraver who made it, we have sought to collect the names of engravers on existing watch papers. The list of engravers which we have been able to compile from various collections is as follows:

Nathaniel Hurd (1730–1777); Paul Revere (1735–1818) for Aaron Willard; Amos Doolittle (1754–1832) ; James B. Longacre (1794–1869); William H. Freeman (1812–18); William Hamlin (1772–1869); William Kneass (1780–1840); William G. Mason (1797–1872) ; Benjamin Jones (1798–1845); Peter Maverick (1780–1831); Joseph Perkins (1788–1842); Reed & Bissell (1825–30); William Rollinson (1762–1842) ; Abraham Simmons (1781–1815); Charles Simons (1820); Samuel Stiles (1796–1861); William F. Stratton (1803–1846); John V. W. Throop (1835); Robert Tiller, Jr. (1818–1835) ; Andrew C. Trott (1779–1812); Elias J. Whitney (1800–1859); Charles C. Wright (1821–1854); John Scoles (1790–1797); A. T. Goodrich (1812–1820); R. M. Gaw (1829–1840) ; James Akin (1793–1846); R. Fairman (c. 1800); Abner Reed (1771–1866); Jocelyn (1796–1881); J. W. Barber (1798–1885); J. W. Orr (c. 1870) ; W. King (?); G. Robb (?); William W. Warr (c. 1830); A. Daggett; S. Atkins; Eddy.

III

Nursery Antiques

Boy with toy horse. Joseph W. Stock c. 1845. COURTESY NEW YORK
HISTORICAL SOCIETY.

Children's Rattles, Pottery Banks and Blow Birds

RATTLES and bells to ward off danger and disease were used by pagan peoples. They also found their way into the ceremonies of the Christian Church and have been used as toys and amulets for children almost since the beginning of time. Many of the early rattles were of terra cotta, but the earliest that seem to relate to the present-day child's rattle were those made of gold, silver and precious stones. In the seventeenth and eighteenth centuries, there were beautiful gold and silver rattles made in European countries in the shape of lions, sea horses, mermaids, eagles and other birds and ships. These had bells on them and were fastened to a chain and attached to the child's belt. Not every child had rattles of this sort, but few of those made of less precious materials seem to have survived.

Mention of American rattles is made in the newspapers of the eighteenth century. Here they are referred to as "whistles and bells," and they were usually imported from England. The earliest mention is by John Pennefather, Goldsmith, who records the robbery of "a child's whistle and chains" in the South Carolina *Gazette,* November 16, 1738. In the

Child's silver rattle with bells and coral handle. American, c. 1760.
COURTESY MUSEUM OF THE CITY OF NEW YORK.

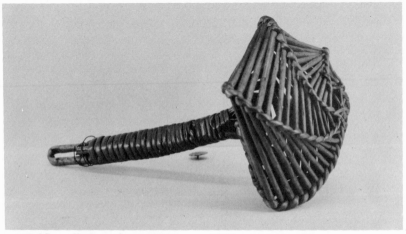

Child's willow rattle. American, c. 1835. COURTESY MUSEUM OF THE
CITY OF NEW YORK.

*Cream stoneware bank. American, 19th
century.* COURTESY NEW YORK
HISTORICAL SOCIETY.

Pennsylvania Journal, March 17, 1763, Philip Syng, Brass Founder, advertises for sale: "A neat gilt silver whistle and corel with eight bells." Edward Milne, Goldsmith and Jeweler, advertises in the same paper, December 15, 1763 and November 8, 1764: "Silver whistles and bells, with corals, chased and plain," and "C. & P. whistles and bells." These were imported from London. Richard Humphrey's advertisement in the *Pennsylvania Evening Post,* August 19, 1777: "Coral and bells for children, gum sticks for ditto."

The gumsticks were for teething and were the forerunner of the teething ring. They were of coral, crystal, ivory, carnelian, agate, bone or mother-of-pearl, and usually had a silver whistle at one end. It would seem some jewelers made rattles to order, for they advertise: "Corals for children's whistles as well as children's whistles and bells." By 1782, Richard Sauce, Hardware, Jewelry and Cutlery, was advertising: "Silver correls, rattles and cawls for children," and John Mason has imported "rattles" among his curious assortment of toys, which also included: "Drest dolls, Naked ditto, and Wigs for Dolls." Wherever they were made, there are quite a few of these silver corals and bells to be found today.

You can buy them in silver shops in this country and abroad, but you can also see them in museum collections. The Yale University Art Gallery has a coral-and-bells rattle made by Daniel Christian Fueter, and one in the Metropolitan Museum is by Nicholas Roosevelt. The rattle in the Sterling and Francine Clark Institute in Williamstown, Massachusetts, was made by the silversmith George Ridout of New York in the mid-eighteenth century.

However, the rattles that are of particular interest to the collector today are the wooden and tin rattles made between

1825 and 1900. The wooden kind are square or rectangular and are usually glued or fitted together. They are varnished or painted and have pebbles or grains of corn inside. Tin rattles were round or rectangular, with a drum-shaped or mallet head and a hollow handle. Some were embossed with the alphabet, an eagle, the phrase, "For a Good Child," or a floral design. They were painted bright red, orange and yellow. Revolving drum-shaped rattles between shafts of twisted wire were made around 1900. Tin balls were also put on bone or wooden handles, and sometimes tin bells were attached to a napkin ring.

Recorded in a scrapbook in the Bella C. Landauer Collection is a bill of September 5, 1854, to Abraham Borger, who bought one dozen tin rattles from W. M. Tiers & Company. Rubber rattles were sold by E. F. Horsman in 1886, and Hurst Purnell & Company, Baltimore, advertised at about the same date: "Tin and metal Rattles at 25¢, 38¢, 75¢, $1.50 and $2 to $6 per doz. India rubber rattles $1.75 to $3.50 per doz. Wood rattles 37¢ to 75¢ per doz."

The silver rattles and teething rings made late in the nineteenth century replaced coral sticks with mother-of-pearl. The straight handles were topped with a dog's head, a rabbit's head or a jester's head with bells. These were also often embossed with scenes and nursery rhymes. In 1900, the firm of Graff, Washbourne & Dunn of New York manufactured rattles and teething rings with Santa Claus, a clown, Bo-Peep and Man-in-the-Moon designs. There were also birthstone teething rattles; they were rings of ivory or mother-of-pearl with bells, the name of the month, the flower of the month and the birthstone of the month. These are rarely found. In 1872, celluloid rattles were invented but few were made

Children's tin rattles. American, c. 1840–1850. COURTESY HENRY FORD MUSEUM.

before 1900. These celluloid balls with handles are still made, but plastic rattles of popular present-day comic figures are more common.

POTTERY BANKS

Molded pottery banks with a cutout money slit in the top or side were made in rural potteries in New England, Pennsylvania and Ohio from the mid-eighteenth to the late nineteenth century. These banks are of red earthenware with a yellow, orange or brown glaze, of cream and gray stoneware, and of brown Rockingham ware. The ordinary ones are round, beehive, box or jug shape, with a handle and a molded knob or finial on top. Sometimes the glaze is mottled or spotted, and the gray stoneware may have painted cobalt-blue decoration.

There were also lion, bird and dog banks and larger book banks. Of the dog banks, poodles and greyhounds were the most popular. There were also brown mottled Saint Bernard dogs with brandy flasks. A red earthenware lion lying on a base was also made, but bird banks such as hens were more popular than dogs or lions. Some banks had small birds on top as a finial. R. C. Remmey, the Philadelphia potter, made banks of gray stoneware with bird finials as late as 1880. Bennington banks were made of Rockingham and flint enamel in various shapes. There was a small chest of drawers, a cottage and a bottle-shaped bank made of Rockingham ware. A bottle with button top and an Uncle Sam head is made of flint enamel, and a brown slip-covered stoneware bank has a steeple top and is marked with the owner's name, "Eddie Norton." A log-cabin bank was also made in brown slip-

Pottery whistle, peacock. Pennsylvania, late 18th century. COURTESY PHILADELPHIA MUSEUM OF ART.

Pottery whistles, cock and hen. Pennsylvania, late 18th century. COURTESY PHILADELPHIA MUSEUM OF ART.

Lion bank, red earthenware. American, 19th century. COURTESY NEW YORK HISTORICAL SOCIETY.

Pottery bank, brown with cream-and-green glaze. American, 19th century. COURTESY NEW YORK HISTORICAL SOCIETY.

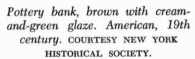

covered stoneware. These banks were made between 1847 and 1877. Many of them are crude in workmanship but they all have an unsophisticated beauty and charm.

Bird whistles or blow birds, as they are called, show more imagination than the banks. There was a small hole in the bird's tail, which sounded a single note. Birds were made of the same red earthenware and stoneware as the banks, but the coloring of the slip was more definite, and such combinations as brown and yellow or yellow and green are often found. Hens and ducks were popular birds, but there were roosters, geese, a yellow canary, a rare peacock and a bird on a nest. Dog and squirrel whistles were also made and a rare figure of a man on a house. A later whistle was made in the form of a teapot. It, like other late whistles, lacks the charm of the earlier Rockingham and stoneware models.

Considering that these banks and whistles were made as toys for children, it is remarkable that so many exist today. Of course, nineteenth-century children were more controlled and better behaved than children today. However, these banks and whistles are not plentiful and the prices are going up constantly. The finest are in museums, not only in regional museums such as Old Sudbury and Shelburne Village, but also in the Metropolitan Museum of Art, the Brooklyn Museum and the Philadelphia Museum of Art. Such toys were also made at English and Continental potteries, but they were not as crude as the American banks and whistles, although they too have an unsophisticated charm.

American Wooden Folk Toys

Toys whittled by the village carpenter or the itinerant carver were favorites with children in early America. These toys were simply designed and crudely carved, but they have an abstract quality which relates them not only to primitive sculpture but to much of the work of contemporary sculptors. Paintings of American children give us a record of some of these toys.

The girl is usually shown with a favorite doll, the boy with a toy wagon, wheelbarrow or hobbyhorse. A boy with a toy wagon painted by Joseph Stock is in Colonial Williamsburg, and a painting in the Maxim Karolik collection in the Boston Museum of Fine Arts shows Warren Crosby with his toy wagon. A portrait of a boy with a hobbyhorse on wheels by Joseph Stock is in the New York Historical Society, and a boy dressed in a plaid outfit sits beside a white hobbyhorse on runners in the painting in the Abby Aldrich Rockefeller Folk Art collection in Colonial Williamsburg.

Many early wooden folk toys were made in New England or Pennsylvania. Carved wooden dolls are formidable in appearance and seem more interesting as folk sculpture than as playthings. Several of these have been found that were carved in New Hampshire. Some old dolls had carved wooden heads set on rag bodies. These were made by local carvers as far west as Ohio and Utah.

Later in the century there were jointed wooden dolls. The arms and legs were pegs joined to the body, but when they were dressed, they could be quite elegant. The heads were turned in the local carpenter's shop.

There were also handmade wagons, children's chairs, chests of drawers and other pieces of furniture for the use of the child, the doll or the doll's house. And there were smaller wooden toys such as clowns, monkeys and hens that jiggled on a string, small wooden merry-go-rounds, caged animals, primitive fire engines, railroad trains and battleships.

The majority of these toys were carved by unknown artisans who whittled their way from house to house. However, a few of these carvers were known and their names have come down to us. An old Swiss named George Huguenin was an itinerant carver in Pennsylvania in the late nineteenth century. He carved stables and barnyard animals such as sheep, cattle, horses, hens and roosters, but sheep were his favorites. They were made of one piece of wood with legs and tails added, and the body covered with pelt. Huguenin also carved small houses, barns and churches, and made Christmas crèche or *putz* figures.

Carved Noah's Arks and Gardens of Eden were also popular in the nineteenth century. They were known as Sunday toys. The Noah's Arks included such wild animals as lions, giraffes, elephants and zebras. A carved Noah's Ark belonging to Katharine Prentis Murphy is in the New York Historical Society. It has 300 small figures of people and animals. Although it is perhaps the finest example of a Noah's Ark ever made, the carver is unknown. There are also small carved

*Hobbyhorse. American, late 18th cen-
tury.* COURTESY NEW YORK
HISTORICAL SOCIETY.

*Painted wooden horse pull toy. American,
mid-19th century.* COURTESY NEW YORK
HISTORICAL SOCIETY.

horses, spotted dogs and the jointed dachshund, and carved and painted wooden birds. Most of these animals were carved with a jackknife and the edges smoothed with a piece of glass. Pine wood was used and some were stained or painted.

The best-known carver of folk animals was William Schimmel (*c.* 1817–1890), a Pennsylvania German. He roamed about the countryside carving roosters, parrots, dogs, squirrels, lions, tigers and eagles. His carving was bold, crudely whittled, and painted strong colors—black, red, yellow or green. Schimmel made a few Hessian soldiers and flower pieces, as well as a Crucifixion scene and Adam and Eve in the Garden. However, the eagles were the most in demand. These ranged in size from those for the parlor mantel to the large eagle with a three-foot wingspread for a flagpole. They were carved of pine, and the bodies of the large eagles often have the wings attached separately. William Mountz, a pupil of Schimmel's, also carved animals and eagles, but in a smoother style.

Hobbyhorses were the child's favorite toy and are particularly appealing to the collector. Homemade hobbyhorses were made from planks whittled for shape, with legs and heads added separately. While the most of the hobbyhorses in paintings or in shops today date from no earlier than the midnineteenth century, Gideon Cox of Philadelphia advertised hobbyhorses in 1825, and they were probably made much earlier. In Europe, they were made in the seventeenth century.

Of course the first hobbyhorses were the one-of-a-kind made by the local carpenter or chairmaker. One was made by the well-known ship carver of Portsmouth, Woodbury Gerrish, in 1844. It is painted brown, has an upholstered saddle

Painted hand-carved wooden doll. American, 19th century. COURTESY
NEW YORK HISTORICAL SOCIETY.

Painted wooden Noah's Ark. American, 19th century. COURTESY
NEW YORK HISTORICAL SOCIETY.

Rocking horse, painted wood. American, early 19th century. COURTESY NEW YORK HISTORICAL SOCIETY.

Rocking horse. Pennsylvania, early 19th century. COURTESY INDEX OF AMERICAN DESIGN.

and leather ears; the horse's head is set in the rocker and there are no visible legs or body. The early carved horses are plain with simply carved heads and flat legs fastened to platforms with wheels or rockers. They had leather ears, real horse tails and forelocks. The bodies were painted tan, red or gray or dappled with black swirls, to suggest hair. They had leather and metal trappings and usually a carpet upholstered seat. Most horses had their feet fastened to the elipse of the rockers, but an especially large horse was made fastened to a rectangular base with metal supports. Then there were the small seats between two cutout horses set on rockers. These were made for a younger child.

Hobbyhorses were advertised in American newspapers from 1850 to 1880. In 1856, Brown & Eggleston of New York advertised them with carriages, showing one sulky-type carriage with a wheel in front, to which a horse's head was fastened. Snow & Kingman, toymakers of Boston in the midnineteenth century, made rocking horses, cabs and children's furniture.

"J. A. Crandalls Patent Spring Rocking Horse" was advertised in *Harper's Weekly* in 1863. These were large horses with real hair mane and tail. Their hind legs were fastened to a platform with a strong metal spring that allowed considerable movement when the rider gave it momentum.

In addition to the hobbyhorse, there were several sizes of small horses set on platforms with wheels and used as pull toys. The horse was the most popular pull toy, but there were also dogs, cats, chickens, ducks and cows. Wild animals included the elephant, tiger and zebra among other circus animals, and the circus wagon with its caged animals behind bars was also made.

English Pottery and Porcelain
Dogs and Cats

———

T HE ENGLISH have a great regard for domestic animals and evidently those in pottery and porcelain were also held in esteem, for countless numbers of them were made. The earliest dogs and cats were of salt glaze or agateware marbled white and black or brown. There was a pug dog of salt-glaze pottery seated on a rectangular base made in Staffordshire in 1745, and there is also a salt-glaze poodle with brown spots. A seated cat in black-and-white agateware, with spots of blue on its chest, back and ears, was made at about the same date. There are also agateware cats with vertical stripes of dark red, buff and white. One striped salt-glaze cat has a mouse in its mouth; another white one, sitting with its tail curled around its paws, is $5\frac{7}{8}''$ tall and is finely modeled. Most of these early cats are sitting, but one manganese purple cat made in 1750 is lying down. Whieldon made cats in typical mottled green-and-brown pottery. All of these early eighteenth-century dogs and cats are of pottery. They are rare and unmarked. There were more early pottery cats than dogs, and for this reason the salt-glaze or agateware dog is rarer than the cat of the same material, but both are so unusual that they are practically nonexistent except in museum collections.

Beginning with the mideighteenth century, cats and dogs were also made at all English porcelain factories. However, there were more dogs than cats made in porcelain, so the cats are rarer and more expensive. Derby and Rockingham made more than the other factories. One of the earliest porcelain cats was a small 3″ black-and-white figure with a mouse in one paw, seated on a base decorated with sprays of flowers in low relief. It was made at the Chelsea Porcelain Works in 1755. A rare Lowestoft porcelain tabby cat painted in the colors of nature is 2¼″ in height and sits on a round green base. It was made in about 1770. Derby made more cats than any other porcelain works. There is a tortoise-shell cat, 2½″ in height, sitting on a buff base decorated with gold; a small 1¾″ realistic cat on a crimson-and-gilt cushion; a large tabby sitting on a green cushion; and a small white cat with black-and-orange spots curled up on a pink cushion.

Cat groups are rare but Derby made several. There is a cat with a child, and another group of a tabby cat with kitten. Both cat and kitten have collars with gold bells, and they sit on a green cushion decorated with a gold-and-white cord. There is also a group of three cats sitting on cerise-colored tiles. A cat with three kittens and a bowl of milk is on white tiles. This group is made in all white, and also with white and tan and one black kitten. A cat and kitten of tan and white sitting on a green cushion was made at Derby and at Worcester. Worcester also made a tiny white cat set on a white base, and a rare tiger cat realistically painted, sitting on an oval pink base.

Rockingham made a great many different cats. There is a

English porcelain cats. Early 19th century. Top row, left: Rockingham black-and-yellow cat on blue cushion. Center: Derby group of cat and kittens, black, white and orange on white tile base. Right: Worcester cat and kitten, white and orange on green cushion. Lower row, left to right: Rockingham, orange, white and black; Worcester upright tiger cat on pink cushion; Derby spotted black and orange cat on pink cushion; Lowestoft upright pink-and-black cat on round blue-green base; Rockingham black-and-orange cat.

small one that sits on a cerise base; a white one on a white-and-gold base; two on a green base; and another group of two on a blue base. There is a small black-and-orange tabby sitting on a blue-and-gold cushion, and a 3″ tan-black-and-white cat with its tail curled about its body. A black-and-orange cat with spotted tail was made on the same mold in about 1820. Rockingham also made several groups with cats, poodles and doghouses. The Cambrian Porcelain Works at Swansea made a white porcelain cat (1814–1817).

There were also a few cats made around the middle of the century. In 1848 when the Derby factory closed, some of the workmen started a small porcelain works. They made white cats with hollow centers and marked them with blue crowns. A cat of brown-and-yellow slipware was made by Thomas Rathbone & Company, Portobello. Many small cats were also made at Staffordshire potteries, but cats gradually lost their popularity and there were none made as companions for the late nineteenth-century dogs.

The story of porcelain dogs follows much the same pattern as that of cats. The earliest ones were made about the middle of the eighteenth century. In about 1755, Longton Hall made a porcelain seated pug dog on a rectangular base. The dog is spotted, with an underglaze of blue and manganese, and measures 3⅝″ in height. It is marked with crossed "L's" in blue.

Dogs of Chelsea porcelain are usually small in size and are often grouped with other figures. The pug was the favorite, and there is a Chelsea pug with a black muzzle; it is 2⅝″ high and is seated on a cushion. A small white pug dog was made of Bow porcelain. Derby made a beige pug dog on a green base; it is of the 1790 period and is 3½″ high. There

Rockingham porcelain poodles, 1800–1820. COURTESY OTTO M. WASSERMAN.

are many poodles of Derby porcelain, but the one with the pink or blue bag in its mouth has been reproduced. White pugs and poodles seated on dark blue bases were made at Worcester and marked Chamberlain, Worcester, in red ink.

From this time on, cats and dogs were made at all the English porcelain factories, but Derby and Rockingham continued to make more than the others. Dogs were more popular than cats, and for this reason more dogs are available today. Dogs of every breed were made including sporting dogs such as greyhounds, pointers, setters, foxhounds, staghounds, and harriers. There were also Dalmations, spaniels, pugs and poodles. Some dogs were portraits, but most had a quaint appearance, although their coloring was close to nature.

The greyhound and the pug were the most popular in the eighteenth and early nineteenth centuries, but later the poodle and the spaniel became favorites. Some dogs are shown retrieving game and some are beside a tree or doghouse. Single dogs are usually sitting, but where there are two, one dog may be lying down. There are poodles holding baskets in their mouths, begging poodles and poodles wearing top hats. Rockingham made a great many hounds, spaniels and poodles. They made hounds of all sizes and in every attitude. There is a white-and-tan whippet on a green base, and there are red-and-tan hounds and white poodles. There is a tiny Rockingham poodle holding a bone in its mouth; a rare Rockingham dog with pups in a basket; and a matching cat with kittens was also made. The basket is straw color, the blanket green, and the cat tabby.

Rockingham also made many playful groups of cats and poodles. There is a white cat and poodle in a doghouse; a cat and poodle beside a vase; and a little group of a cat with a bird in its mouth and a poodle, white with blue-and-pink decorations. All of these groups were made about 1815–1825. A cat and poodle beside a doghouse covered with blue-and-pink flowers was made at Derby. White poodles with black top hats are standing on their hind legs and were made in 1820. Greyhounds and spaniels were made at Rockingham, and a brown-and-white 4″ poodle sitting on a blue base was also made after 1830. Poodles continued to be made until 1842.

Many small dogs were also made of Staffordshire pottery in the early nineteenth century. A pair of brown-and-white and black-and-white setters on a green cushion with red fringe and tassels date about 1800. There is a later amusing group of a standing dog with a small dog peering out of a barrel. There were also mid-Victorian small pottery spaniels beside their kennels, and tiny pairs of sitting poodles only an inch in height. Staffordshire pottery dogs were made in great quantities between 1820 and 1850, and continued to be made until 1870. The mid-Victorian pottery spaniel dominated the English dog scene for many years.

The vogue for pottery dogs as chimney piece decorations lasted throughout the century. The spaniel, or the Comforter as he was called, was the most popular dog for the mantelpiece. They were made in pairs in five sizes from 3½″ to 18″ in height. They were usually white with colored ears, nose and body spots. The color combinations were black and white, brown and white, and red and white. Sometimes a copper luster replaced the color, and a small collar with gold chain and padlock was painted around the dog's neck. These dogs are seldom marked, and although the most of them

Lead-glazed earthenware cat. Staffordshire Astbury Type, c. 1745. COURTESY METROPOLITAN MUSEUM OF ART.

Salt-glazed stoneware cat. Staffordshire agateware, c. 1745. COURTESY METROPOLITAN MUSEUM OF ART.

Rockingham porcelain poodles, 1800–1820. COURTESY OTTO M. WASSERMAN.

were made around the middle of the century, there is no way to date them exactly. Some smaller dogs with more realistic details were made earlier.

In the latter half of the nineteenth century, flat backs were made in two-piece molds by Sampson Smith at Longton until 1878. They were also made at other small potteries in England and Scotland. These were the cheapest sort of pottery. Poodles with "fur" made of shredded clay were also made in Staffordshire potteries but are usually called "Rockingham." This same type of poodle was made at Bennington, Vermont, of flint enamel and Parian marble in 1848.

Cat and dog collecting can be a very expensive hobby. Because the early ones were made as toys or whimsies, they were not considered valuable enough to treasure. Thus there are comparatively few available and the prices have skyrocketed in the last twenty-five years. As we have said, cats are the most expensive. Most early cats are tabbies. The tiger is rare. Pugs are the rarest of dogs. There are many hounds and poodles, and the late large pottery spaniels are cheap and available.

IV

Miniatures

American miniature kitchen. Late 18th century. COURTESY METRO-
POLITAN MUSEUM OF ART

Silver Miniatures

ENGLISH, DUTCH AND AMERICAN

SILVER MINIATURES are a favorite collector's item today. A group of silver miniatures is decorative and fascinating for a cabinet or even for a mantel shelf. These tiny pieces have a special appeal. Since they are expensive and hard to come by, they belong in the field of serious collecting. Miniature silver such as candlesticks, furniture, and tea sets were made for dollhouses in the seventeenth and eighteenth centuries. Nevertheless, not many pieces were made even in the eighteenth century, and the old pieces are very rare today.

Silver miniature pieces include all types of articles in use in the period, as well as a number of pieces seldom found in full size. There is considerable variety in the size of miniature silver articles, since no particular scale was adhered to. The size of some articles indicates that they were made for use in dollhouses, while others such as a mug or porringer and some candlesticks may have been made for the use of the children. Early English and American silver miniatures are especially rare, but there are many Victorian miniatures and reproduction Dutch miniatures on the market today. However, English silver has hallmarks which give us the maker, date and place of manufacture.

Antique Dutch miniatures are desirable, but they are not as rare as the English, since many more of them were made. However, they are scarce enough to be valuable to the collector. Present-day fakes have the same marks and stamps, and such miniatures as sleighs, cabinets, tables, bureaus, chairs and clocks are reproduced. Dutch miniature silver was made by the Leenwarden Silversmiths of Friesland in the fifteenth, sixteenth, and seventeenth centuries, and these miniatures are especially valuable. By the seventeenth century, the silversmiths of Amsterdam and Haarlem and other cities were also making miniatures, and most of the Dutch miniature silver in collections today was made in Amsterdam in the eighteenth or nineteenth century. Dutch marks such as the lion, crowned key, stork, mermaid, fish, horn, deer, goat, acorn, harp, swan and rabbit are easily distinguishable from English silver marks. There is usually the mark of the date and city as well. However it is so difficult to read the Dutch hallmarks that it is almost safer to judge the dates from the style of each piece.

Dutch silver miniatures include teapots, complete tea sets, teaspoons, vases, trays, candlesticks, bowls, furniture such as chairs, tables, cabinets and sleighs, coaches, ships, figures and other toys. Silver toys were also made in Italy as early as 1683, and jeweled toys were made for the children of the court of France in the eighteenth century. Many such toys were made for grownups and given as gifts to be displayed in cabinet collections. These toys include sleighs, coaches and ships of minute workmanship.

The Metropolitan Museum of Art owns a collection of miniature silver filigree toys made in South Germany in the late seventeenth century. It includes furniture such as chairs,

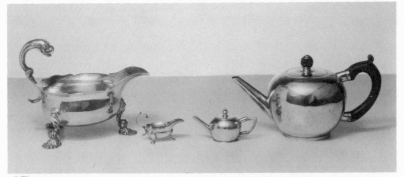

Miniature gravy tureen and teapot, George Middleton. COURTESY
PHILADELPHIA MUSEUM OF ART.

*Miniature silver posset cup, "M.A." London, 1700. Tankard, George
Middleton, London, 1690.* COURTESY PHILADELPHIA MUSEUM OF ART.

*Miniature silver caster, "I.B." London, 1695. Basket, S. Herbert & Co.,
London, 1758.* COURTESY PHILADELPHIA MUSEUM OF ART. (*Large
articles shown for contrast in size.*)

beds, a chest on legs and a child's cradle, as well as vases, candlesticks, a chandelier, a bird cage and a tiny spinning wheel, roasting spit, sleigh and carriage. It is all of intricate design and workmanship. Many similar pieces of silver furniture are reproduced today. Antique silver miniatures are found in the old dollhouses in Dutch and German museums.

The making of miniature silver in England also began in the seventeenth century. The earliest-known pieces were made about 1684, and between this date and the middle of the eighteenth century, all the known hallmarked pieces were made. Most of these were by a few silversmiths who, in addition to making many larger pieces of silver, also specialized in the making of miniatures which—at least in the case of Augustin Courtauld—were marked differently from their larger pieces.

The earliest miniatures are usually marked with four marks on the main body of the article and two marks on the minor parts of the pieces. At a later date, complete marking of small pieces was not required and many of these have only two marks or none at all. The more complete the marks, the greater the value. Many early pieces are fairly crude, but the real value of a miniature is in its rarity, charm and character, not in its technical perfection. The majority of the marked pieces of the eighteenth-century English silver miniatures were made by a few London silversmiths.

There were five English silversmiths who made most of the silver miniatures: George Middleton 1684–1697; M.A. 1697–1715; John Clifton 1703–1715; Augustin Courtauld 1708–1730; and John le Sage 1720–1740.

George Middleton is the earliest and most important of the English silver miniature makers. His pieces are the rarest of all English miniature silver, though fairly crude in work-manship—a characteristic typical of all early miniatures. How-ever, these pieces are fully hallmarked. In addition to teapots of several types, cream and sugars, bowls, posset pots, por-ringers, beakers, tankards and montieth bowls, Middleton made candlesticks, snuffers, spoon racks with trifid spoons and silver stills. He also made sets of miniature chairs in the style of Charles III, with caned backs and seats, and grates complete with firedogs, fender, shovel and tongs. When there is any decoration, it is crudely incised and the design is of leaves and scrolls. The spoons and snuffers measure about 2″ in length, and the teapots less than 2″ in height. Besides those in private collections, the Philadelphia Museum of Art owns a fine collection of silver miniatures by George Middleton and others.

The mark "M A" appears on quite a few pieces of minia-ture silver, but the exact maker's name has not been deter-mined. Pieces with this mark include kettles and braziers, saucepans on stands, tea caddies, coffeepots, jugs, teapots, silver flagons and two-handled silver posset cups with covers and gadroon-and-leaf decoration.

John Clifton made many different types of articles includ-ing fireplaces, cruets and complete tea sets with tiny handle-less cups and teaspoons.

Augustin Courtauld was the most prolific of all English silver-miniature makers. Dollhouses reached their height of popularity during his period (1708–1740), and Courtauld made many varieties of furnishings for them including tables, fireplace sets, sconces, candlesticks and snuffers, bottles, distaffs, watering cans, candlesticks and bed warmers, as well as cruets, saucepans, chocolate pots, covered cups, plates, saltcellars, tea sets complete with trays, tea caddies, tea-spoons and kettles on stands. His pieces are plain and lack the character of earlier miniatures. Courtauld's miniatures are similar to the Dutch miniatures made in Amsterdam at about the same dates, and some with his marks also have Amsterdam stamps as well. Courtauld's miniatures are never completely hallmarked, but are nevertheless valuable and interesting. He used several marks, but his mark on toy silver is always "ac" in small Gothic letters.

In craftsmanship, the miniature pieces of John le Sage are superior to all other silver miniatures, and their construction is comparable to the best full-sized silver pieces. There are not many pieces by le Sage to be found, although he worked over a long period. Pieces include silver trays, tea caddies, sauce boats and silver saltcellars of several types.

Although the makers listed above made the most of the English silver miniatures, some were also made by John Buckle, T. Sympsone, W. H., I. D., William Fleming (child's miniatures), John Cafe, Edward Medleycott, S. Herbert, Charles Wright, C. S. & F. S., C.F.T., Isaac Malyn, John Sotro, Edward Jones, Jonathan Bradley, Matthew Madden, John Cole and Joseph Smith. The word toy had a different meaning in the eighteenth century than it does today, and although no silver miniatures have been found with their marks, undoubtedly many men who are listed as goldsmiths, jewelers, or toymakers did make such toys as silver furnishings for dollhouses. The following were listed as toymen: Francis & Thomas Harrache, Sir Ambrose Heal, Evans, Paul Daniel Chenevix, Lewis Pantin, Edward Flower, John De Crez and William & Mary Deard. It seems only reasonable that the verse, "Farewell to Deards and all her toys which glitter in

Dutch and English silver miniatures. COURTESY CURRIER
GALLERIES.

her shop," refers to something nearer the heart than a pair of shoe buckles, a watch or a snuffbox.

Auction sale records listed by J. W. Caldicott in *Values of Old English Silver and Sheffield Plate* include miniature candlesticks of eighteenth-century design with baluster-shaped stems and octagonal or hexagonal bases, sometimes with shell decorations or gadroon borders and often with a floral chased design. These candlesticks have been found with marks of various makers including John Cory (1712), Gabriel Sleath (1716) and such unidentified makers as I.A. and M.e. Sheffield-plate miniature candlesticks of Corinthian column design were made about 1773.

Miniature goblets from 2⅝" to 4½" in height were made by a number of different English makers of the seventeenth and eighteenth centuries. Miniature mugs and porringers with embossed bands and spiral fluting and molded scroll handles were made by William Andrewes in about 1700, and miniature porringers 2½" in size with *repoussé* decoration were made about the same date by Timothy Ley and Nathaniel Lock, and a little later by Richard Gosling.

Shallow miniature bowls with scrolled wire handles and centers embossed with flowers in punched dotted circles and with fluted and embossed foliage were also characteristic miniature silver pieces of the seventeenth century, although they were usually not dollhouse size. Miniature silver-gilt teaspoons were made by Andrew Archer in 1703, and miniature trays, circular, oval and oblong with fluted borders and with pierced and beaded galleries, were made in the eighteenth century. Miniature teapots and tea sets are particularly interesting. These were made by many silversmiths including

*Miniature silver tea set marked: "C.S. & F.S." and
hallmarks c. 1820.* COURTESY NEW YORK
HISTORICAL SOCIETY.

*South German miniature silver with repoussé filigree decoration
(1675–1700).* COURTESY METROPOLITAN MUSEUM OF ART.

Paul Lamerie (1728), as well as by those already mentioned and many unidentified makers such as "T.P."

A pair of sugar tongs in the Boston Museum of Fine Arts was made by Jeffrey Griffiths of Chester in about 1750. In the New York Historical Society collection is a tea set of fluted Queen Anne design marked "C.S. & F.S." and with hallmarks which date it between 1830 and 1840. The Children's Museum of Hartford, Connecticut, owns a similar tea set on a galleried tray which is marked "C.F.T." and has hallmarks which place it about 1810. A detailed search of every museum would undoubtedly bring to light many more pieces of miniature silver and many more makers' names.

Miniature silver was also made by American silversmiths, although none specialized in the making of miniatures. American silver miniatures are even rarer than those of England. Paul Revere is credited with the making of miniature silver, but none has come to light. There is a set of six miniature teaspoons in the Boston Museum of Fine Arts which are attributed to Richard Richardson of Philadelphia. A small cake basket with pierced rim was made by Zachariah Brigden of Boston (1734–1787), and a miniature teapot made about 1786 by Samuel Bartlett of Boston is in the Yale Museum of Fine Arts. Dolls' teaspoons were made by William I. Jenney (1831–1852), by Howard & Company, New York (1860–1940), and by Dueme & Company. In the 1870's, Roswell and Bradbury Bailey of Vermont were making miniature teaspoons, and undoubtedly a great many other American silversmiths made a few miniature spoons or tea sets on special order. The Museum of the City of New York owns a miniature tea set made by Gorham in 1920.

Besides the modern Dutch miniatures, silver miniature tea

sets were made in Japan, and are still being made in England and by American silver companies. Those made in Japan are so marked and are attractive and of comparatively good workmanship. Completed miniature silver tea sets are rare. Such pieces as a cruet stand, a sauce boat, a cake basket, saucepan with wooden handle, or a spill spoon are especially rare.

Pottery and Porcelain Miniatures

Mᴵɴɪᴀᴛᴜʀᴇ ᴅɪsʜᴇs of various sizes have been made by European potteries since the sixteenth century. Along with other tiny household articles, pottery and porcelain was a necessary part of the furnishings of dollhouses. Pottery jugs, mugs, jars and pans were made to furnish the kitchen, where they were arranged on hanging shelves or cabinets, and tea sets and dinner sets were made for the dining room, while pairs of porcelain vases were for the decoration of mantels and cabinets in other rooms.

Many varieties of miniature pottery and porcelain were made for European children, for the adult cabinet collection, and for use in dollhouses. The earliest miniature pottery was that made for the Nürnberg kitchens in German dollhouses in the sixteenth and seventeenth centuries. Nürnberg pottery with hand-painted floral designs and a glaze similar to majolica was made as early as 1550. Plates, bowls and covered jugs and mugs were in miniature, as well as pottery tile stoves. The design of Nürnberg pottery included birds, fruit, flowers, arabesque borders, and portrait busts and religious subjects in relief. The pottery base was usually green or white enamel, and the colors were brilliant blue, yellow, green or manganese. Rhemish stoneware mugs and jugs with silver mounts were also made in miniature for German dollhouses of the seventeenth century.

Early miniatures of Chantilly and Mennecy porcelain were made for dollhouses in the time of Louis XV. Early Dutch dollhouses have Chinese porcelain vases and bottles placed in rows on mantel shelves. Chinese porcelain miniature vases are represented in Chinese paintings as early as the fourteenth century. Early miniature vases were made in powder blue, *sang de boeuf*, peach bloom and yellow porcelain. Black was also a favorite for miniature sets. Small saucers and vases in blue and white measuring 1½" date from the K'ang Hsi period. Miniatures were also made in *famille-rose* designs. The earliest English dollhouses had miniature Chinese porcelain vases, usually blue and white, and bowls and plates of Lambeth delft. Rows of covered flagons stand on cupboard shelves or hang on wall racks in miniature kitchens and dining rooms.

Philip Elers, the Dutch potter who introduced salt glaze into English potteries, may have made some of this for dollhouses. A miniature salt-glaze tea set with raised figures is in the collection of the British Museum, and salt-glaze mugs, washtubs and bleeding cups were made for eighteenth-century English dollhouses. One such dollhouse has a Welch dresser with rows of miniature creamware—some in blue-and-white willow pattern and some with a blue feather edge. Swiss porcelain with floral decoration was also made for eighteenth-century dollhouses, and a German doll's kitchen of the period has crockery of Künersberger ware (1745–1770). This is decorated with freehand floral designs in blue and white or yellow and green. It is similar to Rouen pottery, and

Child's spatterware tea set, 19th century. COURTESY
NEW YORK HISTORICAL SOCIETY.

Miniature porcelain. Left, Coalport; right, Spode. COURTESY
D. M. & P. MANHEIM.

Dolls' tea set. Tea-leaf pattern, 19th century. COURTESY
NEW YORK HISTORICAL SOCIETY.

the designs are both Oriental floral and pastoral scenes. Tiny porcelain bowls and vases with flowers in red and mauve were made at Limbach in the late eighteenth century and marked "L." Miniature porcelain vases also were made in Thuringian potteries.

Many English potteries made dishes for dollhouses of the eighteenth century and later. They also made miniature dishes of several sizes for children's and dolls' use, as well as the tiny-scale dollhouse miniatures. Small sauce boats of Bow porcelain with roses and powder-blue decoration were made as early as 1759. Whieldon made miniature tea sets in brown and white and mottled ware. Leeds Pottery miniature tea sets and dinner sets with feather-edge, hand-painted borders such as the wheat pattern, willow transfer decoration and pierced decoration, were also made in miniature. Pottery cake molds of Leeds Pottery or Wedgwood were popular. Lusterware tea sets and vases in miniature, and tiny Staffordshire hens on nests, sheep and other figures were made as well. Staffordshire plates with designs of children rolling a hoop and flying a kite while Grandfather looked on are identical with the scenes found on children's mugs of the same date. Hand-painted miniature sets with black decoration were made at Caughley.

Porcelain miniatures include tiny teapots and pap boats made of Derby and Coalport porcelain. These have naturalistic designs such as carnations, roses and blue convolvulus raised in relief, and painted flowers and butterflies on mauve, yellow or green grounds. Tiny miniature candlesticks painted with flowers and birds were made at Swansea, Spode and other potteries of the eighteenth and early nineteenth centuries. Rockingham, Spode and Worcester also made miniature porcelain dolls' sets with gold and bright colors.

Spode made miniature pottery tea and dinner sets with blue transfer Oriental designs. A dinner set has meat dishes 6″ in length and cheese plates 1½″ in diameter. The soup and sauce ladles have the transfer design in their bowls. Transfer patterns include one of a milkmaid and cows, with a rose border in blue and white, a pattern of fruit and flowers, and an Oriental design of birds. Wedgwood miniatures include transfers in one color such as the blue-and-white Willow pattern and transfers of exotic birds printed in apple green and other colors. These have 2″ cups.

In the early part of the nineteenth century, miniature tea sets with painted decoration and pink transfers were made at Lowestoft. A Lowestoft tea set with pink transfers of scenes of mother and child, and a set with landscape transfers and gold borders, were used by Queen Victoria as a child. Victoria also had a miniature Leeds tea set.

Miniature dishes of Chinese export porcelain were probably made to order. One such tea set has a design of painted hearts flaming upon an altar in black and gold, and dates to 1780. In 1810, a Chinese porcelain miniature set was made with transfer scenes from the English engraving of Bartolozzi's "Playing at Marbles." Many of these sets have tea caddies and cups, both with and without handles. However, many of these sets, while miniature in size, were for children themselves.

In the early nineteenth century, Davenport made miniature tea and dinner sets in blue-and-brown transfer and in flowing blue and brown colors. Miniature sets of mochaware, spatterware, plain white ironstone and tea-leaf-patterned ironstone and sprig china were also made at that time. Old

Child's tea set. Black transfer scenes of mother and child. COURTESY
FRANCIS PEEK, LTD., NASSAU, BAHAMAS.

Child's blue-and-white Worcester tea set. COURTESY
ARTHUR ACKERMAN.

Nankin and Staffordshire transfers with children were popular designs on miniature sets of the era. A brown transfer series which included the design, "A Prize for Sewing Well," is to be found on 2″ plates which are smaller than cup plates. There were also miniature tea sets of pink luster with teapots only 2¾″ high.

Toy dishes of Dresden and Limoges porcelain were made for dollhouses in the nineteenth century, but the most common dollhouse dishes were a heavy china with blue-and-pink floral designs and gold borders, and dollhouses of 1860 and after were usually furnished with this type of dishes. However, miniature dishes also continued to be made in Germany, and complete kitchen crockery sets of Meissen onion pattern were made late into the nineteenth century. Miniature Staffordshire cottage vases and figures of men, women and dogs date from the late nineteenth century. Bowls and pitchers, pairs of miniature spill vases, watering cans, baskets with handles and compotes of porcelain were made by Spode, Rockingham, and others. Pairs of Chinese and Japanese vases were another part of the furnishings of the nineteenth-century dollhouse.

In 1808, there were toy merchants in France who specialized in furniture, china and other articles for furnishing dollhouses, and as late as the Paris Exposition of 1849, dolls' kitchens, shops and houses with pottery and porcelain, complete in perfection of detail, were shown. French toy catalogues pictured collections of iron pots and pans, knives, forks, candlesticks and fireplace equipment, as well as furniture of the Empire period. At the St. Louis, Missouri, Exposition in 1908, French toy manufacturers exhibited toy furnishings.

Queen Mary arranged for the building of a dollhouse which was complete in every detail of twentieth-century furnishings. Miniature dishes for the Queen's dollhouse were made to order by Doulton, Spode, Wedgwood and others. The Doulton dinner set is of bone china decorated with bands of gold, and each piece bears Queen Mary's royal crest with the monogram "M.R." (Mary Regina). These pieces were made in scale to fit the size of the rooms. The exhibition of this dollhouse revived an interest in miniature articles, and today tiny miniatures are eagerly sought by collectors. Miniature pottery and porcelain is not only collected for the furnishing of dollhouses. There are also collectors who specialize in miniature candlesticks or tea sets.

American dollhouses are not often found with dishes of any value. However, the Metropolitan Museum has a kitchen made late in the eighteenth century which is complete with mottled and freehand painted crockery bowls, stoneware jugs and mugs. Bennington Rockingham jugs, mugs, pitchers, bowls and cooky jars from ¾″ to 2″ in size have also been found. Another American dollhouse of the 1870's has a complete set of kitchenware of Meissen blue-and-white onion pattern of nineteenth-century make, including jugs, mugs, bowls and containers for sugar, flour, salt and other staples.

Anyone looking for articles of miniature pottery or porcelain will have difficulty in finding fine old pieces, but there are many sets which were made in France, Germany or Japan in the early nineteenth century, and now and again a few stray miniature pieces of old European pottery or porcelain are to be found. Porcelain miniatures are also being made today. Generally speaking, dinner sets are rarer than tea sets, and miniature vases and teakettles are also rare. An odd cup or saucer, a watering can or a bowl and pitcher—or for that matter any single piece—is easier to find, while sets are rare. Fine miniatures are expensive and only to be seen in the better shops.

Miniatures in Tin, Pewter, Brass, Copper, Iron and Wood – Miniature Bric-a-Brac

MINIATURE household articles have been of interest to collectors for many centuries. As early as 1572, a tiny kitchen was made, complete with all kitchen utensils in miniature. It consisted of plates, dishes, spoons and egg cups all made of tin. Many articles in the Nürnberg kitchens of the seventeenth and eighteenth centuries were also of tin. These included graters, sieves, strainers and skimmers; pans, funnels, pudding molds, candlesticks and lanterns, as well as many other common and useful articles. American eighteenth-century dollhouse kitchens also included tiny tin pudding molds, candleboxes and candlesticks. In the first half of the nineteenth century, miniature tin fireplace grates and snip tin fireplaces were made, and there were also rare tin shears and sugar tongs. Whether these small articles were made as samples or proofs of skill, they eventually found their way to the child's dollhouse. The early nineteenth-century tin miniatures were also often stenciled or hand painted, and there were tiny Chippendale-shaped trays with floral stencils and stenciled bread servers. There were also miniature tin dustpans, flour scoops and flour bins.

In about 1840, an English kitchen doll was made with voluminous skirts that opened up to reveal a complete set of miniature tin kitchen utensils. The famous pedlar dolls of this era also carried many tin pieces including kitchen utensils, knives and forks, scissors and thimbles. Tin kitchens complete with tin stoves were made late in the nineteenth century both in Europe and in America. A toy kitchen in the Museum of the City of New York was made in 1850 and includes miniature tin pans, buckets, a washtub, dishes, and matchbox, all of tin.

Many early miniatures were also made of copper, brass and pewter. In the old Nürnberg kitchen, there were pewter basins, mugs and measures, pewter spoons, plates, molds, pitchers and many other small articles of pewter. Many of the old Nürnberg miniature pewter pieces have the maker's mark. There are also examples of English and American pewter. Tiny pewter tea services, plates and platters were played with by New York children as early as 1781. Pewter colanders, tea caddies and bleeding cups were used in English eighteenth-century dollhouses. In the nineteenth century, Roswell Gleason is known to have made a miniature pewter tea set for his daughter, and Britannia miniature tea sets like the one in Joseph Stock's portrait of Mary Childs were made in considerable quantities.

Brass miniatures included fireplace tools, kettles, warming pans, plate warmers, scales, bird cages, a solid-brass beaten mortar 1½" high, and rare shell-shaped cake, jelly and pudding molds of brass with tiny rings to hang them by. There were also rings holding miniature brass spoons, key rings with keys to lock the tiny cabinets and dollhouse doors. Small brass candlesticks were made in Queen Anne, Chippendale and later Adam designs, and even in midnineteenth century Victorian shapes. There were also brass candle snuffers, trays and hanging brass chandeliers of early type used in Dutch dollhouses. Brass rarities include a brass bird cage and a tiny mousetrap, a plate warmer and a matchbox.

Miniature copper kettles, coffeepots, saucepans and small iron-handled copper spoons, strainers and ladles, hung around the old hooded chimneys in the miniature eighteenth-century kitchens. An old copper brazier in a Nürnberg kitchen is decorated with a *repoussé* rope pattern. Today many brass and copper miniatures have been reproduced, and the collector must be careful to distinguish between the old and the new.

There were also miniatures of hand-wrought iron and cast iron made for use in dollhouses. Although some fireplaces were made earlier, between 1825 and 1860, many miniature cast-iron fireplaces complete with grates, firebacks and fireplace tools were made by ironworkers in their spare time, and may have been used as samples or made for display on cottage kitchen mantel shelves. But eventually they have found their way into miniature rooms or dollhouses. Rare iron fireplaces of the late eighteenth century have a coat of arms, a lion or a rose or thistle design and sets of firedogs, tongs, fender, coal scuttle and other accessories to match. Other iron fireplaces of the period are in Adam design. These measure 5″ by 6″ up to 8″ by 9″ and are smaller than those made in the nineteenth century, which are often as large as 12″ by 13″. One little fireplace made about 1835 has a design of Masonic emblems; another has a British coat

Toy decorated tinware, iron pots, kettles and andirons. American, early 19th century. COURTESY ESSEX INSTITUTE, SALEM, MASS.

Early 19th-century miniature wooden tea set. Small wooden doll. COURTESY ESSEX INSTITUTE, SALEM, MASS.

Child's Britannia tea set, 19th century. COURTESY CHILDREN'S MUSEUM, HARTFORD, CONN.

of arms. Mid-Victorian miniature fireplaces have steel-and-brass bars and brass trimmings. There were also tiny all-brass fireplaces. The accessories and fireplace equipment included trammels, shovels, spiders or trivets as small as $1\frac{7}{8}''$, irons and iron stands and tongs. In the late nineteenth century, iron stoves were made which were exact reproductions of the well-known patented models, and they had tiny plates with the trade names identical with large stoves. Other iron miniatures include iron skillets with long handles, three-legged pots and heart-shaped trivets. Many spoons, ladles, strainers and scoops were of brass or copper, and had long, hand-wrought iron handles, sometimes with miniscule turned wooden handles at their ends. Chopping knives, roasting forks and shovels also had turned wooden handles. There were tiny wooden bowls and plates, small wooden wallboxes and containers of turned wood, and in the nineteenth century, wooden buckets, wooden coffee grinders and rolling pins and many other wooden cooking and laundry utensils.

Miniature bric-a-brac used in dollhouses included pictures, mirrors, clocks, wall hangings, statues, figurines, vases and numerous other objects such as fans and opera glasses. Miniature mirrors of all periods are to be found, from the early walnut-framed Queen Anne type down to gilt Victorian overmantel mirrors and tall pier glasses. There were also miniature mirror sconces. Tiny tapestries and other wall hangings were woven or painted for early dollhouses, and pictures which are exact copies of old masters are to be found in some of them. There are bits of framed needlework, small engravings framed or sometimes pasted to the walls. Some old dollhouses had copies of family portraits or miniature eighteenth-century carved ivory scenes of ships, seascapes,

Roman ruins, pastorals or scenes from mythology. These plaques were made in Vienna and the Low Countries, and thus are most often found in German or Dutch dollhouses. Many other tiny articles of turned or carved ivory or a combination of ivory and lignum vitae were made in miniature. These include cups, vases, candlesticks, wine coolers and musical instruments. Pieces of miniature furniture were also made entirely of ivory or ornamented with ivory.

Victorian dollhouses had colored lithograph and chromo-lithographed pictures which were sentimental in subject matter and were small reproductions of pictures popular at that time. There were also small marble and ivory statues. The early eighteenth-century miniatures were beautifully executed and are thus valuable today. They include busts of poets, classical busts and tiny Chinese porcelain figures and vases. Later miniature pottery figures were made at Stafford-shire. These include the popular sheep, dogs, hens on nests and figures of shepherds and shepherdesses. There were also later cheap plaster figures including such popular statues as the "Greek Slave." Of course today all kinds of tiny dogs, cats and other figures are available, and one has to be careful not to buy just a cheap imitation.

Miniature clocks of all kinds exist, from the tiny signed clocks made by well-known clockmakers and sometimes found in eighteenth-century English dollhouses to the late steeple-topped American mantel clocks. There were miniature cuckoo and wag-on-the-wall clocks and tiny grandfathers' clocks with carving, inlay, brass trim and painted faces. Most of the old clock miniatures have works in complete working order. Late cheap mantel clocks usually do not have works.

Other interesting accessories include hatboxes complete

with hats, combs, brushes and mirrors; calfskin trunks studded with nails; and household brushes of all sorts. There were also complete sets of miniature table linen and bed linen. The pure-linen table napkins and tablecloths were often hand loomed and fringed. Sheets and towels were hand hemmed and sometimes trimmed with handmade lace; tiny wool blankets were hand woven. In the old dollhouses, all the hand-woven fabrics were small in scale, although they were usually copies of patterns used by grownups. There were also tiny Gobelin tapestries, velvets and stamped leathers for upholstery. Later miniature patchwork quilts were made, and knitted and crocheted lace doilies are often found.

There were miniature baskets of all shapes and sizes measuring ½″ to 4″ or 5″ in length. There were large, deep baskets, flat baskets for bread, vegetable, fruit and flower baskets with handles and tiny basket cradles. There were also strings of baskets of all kinds, both covered and uncovered. Sewing baskets were complete with miniature spools of thread, scissors and thimbles.

Another interesting small article was the miniature book. In an early eighteenth-century Dutch dollhouse, one room known as the Apothecaries' Library has its walls lined with bookshelves filled with leather-covered scientific books. These books were probably made especially for this dollhouse, as were many other miniature books. However, many of them were made for adults, and the collecting of beautifully bound miniature books has been a hobby since the seventeenth century. Some of the books are even illuminated by hand and set in gold and jewels. Foremost among them were the tiny thumb bibles. The *Koran,* the *Meditations of St. Augustine,* the *Book of Hours* and many other religious books were printed in miniature, from a few milligrams to several inches in size. A *Book of Hours* intended for children's use was printed as early as 1625, and there are small books printed for children in English, French, Dutch and German. There are tiny *Fables de la Fontaine, Catechisms for the Young* and many other moral and religious books. There are also tiny animal alphabet books, costume books with costumes of different nations, books of nursery rhymes and A B C's. A miniature Dutch history with copperplates was printed for the instruction of the young in 1753.

In the Dutch dollhouses at the Denver Museum there is a group of tiny books, all leather bound and decorated with gold tooling or blind embossing, and one that is ivory bound. They are printed in Dutch, German and French, and contain engravings and hand decorations. There is also a tiny photograph album with places in which to set pictures, and a Dutch calendar for the year 1803.

In one of the Helena Rubenstein rooms is a *Calendrier de la Jeunesse pour l'an 1805* which contains miniature photographs of French royalty. Another book, *Exercises du Chrétien* was published in Paris in 1733. Miniature books in the eighteenth-century English dollhouse of Ann Sharp include *Aesop's Fables, Emblems of Love* and cards of *Cries of London.* In *Early American Children's Books,* A. S. W. Rosenbach lists "a *Child's Handbook*-toy for a doll's house."

A pedlar doll of about 1840 carries the nineteenth-century novels, *Lady Elizabeth* and *Resolution,* each about ½″ in length. In the Museum of the City of New York, the miniature books include *Scripture Gems,* published in New York in 1836 by Taylor & Gould. This book measures 1″ by 1¼″. The museum also owns a miniature wooden bookcase filled with sixteen volumes of books $2\frac{2}{5}''$ by $1\frac{4}{5}''$. This is called *The Infant's Library* and was published by J. Marshall in 1793, probably as a toy for a dollhouse.

There were many more miniature articles not named here. The Helena Rubenstein collection of miniature rooms alone contains over 20,000 antique objects of silver, gold, ivory, glass, copper, brass, pewter and even semiprecious stones. These include, in addition to the furniture, clocks, mirrors, glass and silver candelabra, writing-desk sets and miniature leather-bound books. These were all made by master craftsmen of France, Italy, England, Germany, Spain, Austria, Holland and America, and thus give an idea of the wide variety of miniature articles made for old dollhouses and toys for grownups to collect.

Miniature Glass Toys

GLASS TOYS have been made since early times and were found among excavations in Egypt and Greece. These may have been made as whimsies, but they were probably made as toys for children to play with. Glass toys were also known in the Middle Ages, and there is a legend of St. Elizabeth which tells of the glass toys which she bought in Eisenach, Germany.

Glass in Dutch and German dollhouses dates from the sixteenth and seventeenth centuries and includes minutely blown mugs, cruets, jugs and bowls in green and amber glass with applied bands, fancy finials and handles, prunts and rigaree decoration. These hand-blown miniatures are in the Italian tradition and may have been made in Italy or by Italian glass blowers working near the toymaking centers in Germany and Holland. In the eighteenth and nineteenth centuries, glass toys such as jugs, glasses and spoons were made in Lanscha, Thuringia, in the glass districts of the Bavarian and Bohemian forests and in Passau. The workmanship of glass toys is often as fine as that of any of the larger pieces of the period.

There are a few rare glass miniatures such as the clear-glass decanter and wineglasses of early eighteenth-century Dutch or English glass which are in a dollhouse of the period in the Victoria and Albert Museum in London. The wineglasses have simple baluster stems and the set is a rare example, since no large decanter sets of the same period have been preserved.

London glass toymakers were known to exist as early as 1696. In 1760, John Bench of Warwick advertised glass toys. John Peploe of Birmingham advertised them in 1765, and in 1772, C. Haedy, a London glass cutter from Germany, advertised "Toys for young Ladies" along with other glass articles. In 1785, Imison and King of Manchester made "all sorts of glass toys in miniature." The making of glass toys was general at first, but by the end of the eighteenth century the industry was centered in Birmingham. In 1801, Owen Johnson and Shakespear & Johnson advertised glass toys, and in the Birmingham directory of 1816 there were ten glass-toy manufacturers listed, while by 1855 there were thirty-two.

It is safe to say that most of the glass tea sets and other miniature pieces called Bristol or Nailsea were made at Birmingham. Certainly both types of glass were made there; the Nailsea glassworks, which also made Bristol-type glass, had a branch at Birmingham after 1824. From the very beginning of glassmaking in Birmingham in the eighteenth century, forgeries of both Bristol and Nailsea were made in Birmingham. Blue and green colored glass and later purple and puce were made. Thomas Osler, the well-known maker of cut glass, also made glass toys in 1811. Bristol-type glass included hand-blown opaque white glass with hand-painted floral decoration, as well as royal blue, green and clear glass. Little tea sets of this type were made in great quantities in 1870–1880 in Birmingham. Tea sets were also made with

*Right: English opaque miniature glass with floral decoration. Left:
German blown-glass miniatures, 19th century.* MISS SCHNEIDER
COLLECTION.

Nineteenth-century miniature glass, Nailsea and Bristol types. MISS
SCHNEIDER COLLECTION.

clear-and-opaque spirals and blue-and-opaque spirals on clear-glass grounds. Tiny glass candlesticks of both baluster and chamber type were made, some in a combination of clear and turquoise glass with bases in applied decoration. Coffee-pots, chocolate pots, mugs, bases and plates were in spiral and plain glass. However, some miniatures were made at Bristol in 1840, and may have been made much earlier—certainly at least a few offhand pieces. A set of six ¾"-high wineglasses in Bristol blue with plain stems and circular feet, a pair of port decanters 1¾" in height, a set of seven tumblers ¾" in height, and two water jugs about 1½" high were advertised by a Birmingham dealer that year.

There were some miniatures made of Nailsea glass. This is characterized by loops and diagonal stripings of white, green or yellow in clear glass. Blue-and-white spiral stripes, and yellow-and-white spiral miniature vases and perfume bottles, were also made. Opaque white stripes on clear-glass vases, and bottles decorated with designs of red-and-green dots, were made in the early eighteenth century. Tiny 2" scent bottles were made to order as love tokens and had a heart, initials and the date inscribed in mauve or red dots on a bottle with opaque striping on a white ground, edged with beads of color. Most of these were made between 1816 and 1824. They are rare and valuable and although not made as toys, are comparatively small in size. Miniatures of Italian blown glass are more plentiful than any other and were made from the sixteenth century down through the present day.

Miniatures of American glass are much rarer than those of European glass. However, miniatures were made at the various American glasshouses, and there are some pieces on the market today. Blown-glass miniatures were made in South

Jersey, New York, and in Midwestern glasshouses, as well as at Sandwich and other New England glasshouses. Tiny blown baluster-stem wineglasses not more than 2″ in height have been found in aquamarine, and mugs less than 2″ high were also made in aquamarine South-Jersey-type glass. Tiny blown creamers in deep cobalt blue and deep green, and South-Jersey-type pitchers with threaded necks, lily-pad decoration and crimped feet, have been found in aquamarine glass. Needless to say, they are rare and although they are minute, they were not made for dollhouses but for a child or as a whimsy. Tiny candlesticks with knobbed stems were also made in dark green and aquamarine South-Jersey-type glass.

Blown three-mold glass miniatures are interesting. A tiny amethyst bowl was blown in a stopper mold and has a diamond pattern, and miniature decanters with geometric diamond ribbing and sunburst designs have been found. A rare canary decanter and a cruet both have sunburst and diamond motifs and were made at Sandwich. Tiny pitchers and cordial glasses were also made at Sandwich. Gothic-arch motifs are found on small footed bowls.

Miniature lacy glass cups and saucers in sapphire blue, and compotes and covered dishes in amethyst, yellow, blue, clear and opal glass, were also made, as well as covered salts, cream and sugars, plates and other dishes. Compotes, bowls and pitchers with lacy flower and festoon designs or flowers in panels and conventional designs and stipplework were also made. Tiny tumblers with conventional designs and diamond points with a star at the base were made in sapphire blue and crystal. These designs are not the same as those found on adult-size lacy glass. In addition to these, bowls, cups and saucers, platters, plates, pitchers and creamers were made about 1830. Besides the flower motifs, shell, scroll, heart and arrow designs were used. These miniatures were probably originally made in sets and were in various colors, as well as in clear, opaque and opal glass.

Miniature pressed glass in Barberry, Saw-tooth, Cable, Honeycomb and Lion patterns were also made. Toy hobnail glass was made by Adams & Company of Pittsburgh after 1880. Small Tiffany-glass vases were tiny enough to be used in a dollhouse. Miniature cut-glass punch bowls and cups were made with fine cutting, but around 1900, cheap cut-glass imitations were popular. In fact, all of these late miniature glass pieces were so cheap when first made that neither child nor parent valued them, and so we find few left today. I remember my tiny toy glass pitcher which somehow escaped breaking and served as a container for cream or syrup on my breakfast tray years after I had discarded dolls and dollhouses.

Any kind of miniature glass gains a certain charm from its diminutive size, and while there is much that is valuable only for its dimensions, there were many fine glass miniatures made.

Complete sets are rare, but individual pieces are often found in present-day shops. Generally, American glass miniatures are the most valuable.

V

Antiques for the Epicure

Heda, still life with swan pie. COURTESY NATIONAL GALLERY, LONDON.

Earthenware Teapots

—————

THE STORY of teapots is not only a commentary on the ceramic industry but also a reminder of more gracious days. In the East, teaism was a cult founded on the adoration of the beautiful among the sordid facts of everyday existence. In 1610, ships of the Dutch East India Company brought the first tea into Europe, and along with it, teapots of stoneware which were copied in Holland and became models for European teapots. The Chinese preferred these in unglazed red or brown stoneware, since they were thought to give a better flavor than those in white porcelain. John Philip Elers, a Dutch potter, made the first redware teapots in Staffordshire, and the first porcelain teapots were made at Meissen, Germany, in 1720. French and English porcelain was soft paste. Tea was expensive, so the first teapots were small.

Some teapots, such as the bundle of bamboo stalks, took their shape from Chinese models, but European teapots as a whole followed the shapes of European silver. However, the twisted handle ending in sprays of leaves and berries was a direct borrowing from the Chinese, and the Chinese flower or dog finials were popular.

Since porcelain was expensive, the eighteenth-century Staffordshire potters preferred to work in white salt-glazed stoneware or brown-and-white earthenware. These teapots were decorated with painted designs or patterns molded, stamped or applied. Red stoneware teapots with relief decoration were made about the middle of the eighteenth century. There were also Whieldon and Astbury types with white clay reliefs of leaves and flowers. The shapes of these early pots were usually simple and utilitarian, with plain watering-can spouts, handles and button finials. Whieldon, and later Wedgwood, also made solid agateware and tortoise-shell teapots with and without relief decoration. These stood on claw feet and the lids had bird or Chinese dog finials.

The first Cauliflower and Pineapple glazed earthenware teapots were also made at this time. There were several different designs of pineapple, cabbage and cauliflower, with the leaves forming the main part of the body and the fruit or vegetable the top third and cover. Some Pineapple pots were rounded, while others had a pineapple set within a baroque cartouche. Cauliflower and Pineapple ware was made in Majolica in the late nineteenth century. Salt-glaze stoneware was decorated with scratched blue designs and with applied decoration, and some teapots were molded in the shape of a house or a camel.

In 1762, Wedgwood perfected the formula for his creamware and this became the important material for teapots. It was also made at Leeds and other Staffordshire potteries. Some creamware teapots had a molded design of horizontal bands and bead borders. The handles were twisted and ended in a cluster of leaves and berries, like handles on Chinese export porcelain. Spouts were curved and molded, and the lids had flower finials. Other creamware teapots were painted with overglaze enamels in shades of green, dull red and violet.

Staffordshire red stoneware teapot with relief decoration. Mid-18th century. COURTESY METROPOLITAN MUSEUM OF ART.

English glazed earthenware teapot, cauliflower form, cream and green. COURTESY METROPOLITAN MUSEUM OF ART.

Staffordshire salt-glazed stoneware teapot in form of a house. Mid-18th century. COURTESY METROPOLITAN MUSEUM OF ART.

Whieldon-type teapot of glazed agateware. Cream with blue, black, yellow and brown veining. English mid-18th century. COURTESY METROPOLITAN MUSEUM OF ART.

Leeds pottery teapot with transfer print, 18th century. COURTESY METROPOLITAN MUSEUM OF ART.

The designs were Chinese subjects—flowers, birds and insects. Still other creamware teapots were transfer printed in black with such designs as Harlequin and Columbine, the Prodigal Son, the Tea Party and Birds—all rare Leeds or Wedgwood. There was also a rare Leeds teapot with the inscription "Speed the Plow." It has a twisted handle and a convolvulus finial. Wedgwood and Leeds also made teapots decorated with commemorative black transfer designs. Both sent their teapots to Sadler and Green at Liverpool for decoration, so both often have the same Liverpool transfer designs.

There are enough different kinds of Wedgwood teapots to limit a collection to Wedgwood ware alone. Besides the early Whieldon types such as Tortoise Shell and Cauliflower, there are the Black Basalts. A Black Basalt teapot with a wicker handle has the seated figure of a widow for a knob. Other Black Basalts were decorated with molded designs, and some had encaustic painted decoration. Then there are the jasperware teapots—blue and white, green and white, lavender and white, and drab and cholocate, with applied classic decoration. All of these were first made in the late eighteenth century, but many are still being made, so that it is necessary to be careful and deal only with authorized dealers when buying expensive items. About 1830 Wedgwood made stoneware teapots of low squat design with an allover molded decoration called Patrician. It had a dog finial. This and other molded dry-body teapots were first illustrated in Wedgwood's 1817 catalogue. In the 1830's this firm also made various designs of the popular colored transfer-printed ware.

Luster was first made in the late eighteenth century. It was produced in great quantities in the Staffordshire potteries at

Bristol, Leeds, Sunderland and Swansea by the nineteenth century. It was made for cottage use, but today really good luster is expensive. Luster teapots are rarer than jugs. There are many types in gold, silver and copper. Blue and silver and canary and silver are the most sought after and rarest colors. Various techniques were used in luster decoration: some is plain, some molded in relief, some painted, stenciled, printed or treated in resist. Resist luster is rarer than other types.

The patterns include tropical birds and foliage and grape-and-leaf designs. Luster imported to America was advertised in the Boston *Columbian Sentinel* May 17, 1820: "Blue-printed lustre, green-sprig lustre oval tea sets, rosebud lustre, drab lustre jugs." Pink Sunderland luster is less sophisticated and the patterns have a folk-art quality. The Cottage pattern painted in green on a pink luster ground is typical. There were many makers of luster but few pieces are marked. It is still being made in the old patterns and on the old molds, so the buyer must beware. The most important thing about luster is the decoration; if it is a good design and in good condition, the piece is worth owning.

In November 1820, the following china was unloaded at Boston: "150 packages mostly Ridgways-Blue printed dining services, British and Turkish scenery, Blind Boy, Stag and Willow patterns." (Boston *Columbian Sentinel,* November 1, 1820.) Other patterns of printed pottery advertised in American newspapers at about this time included British scenery, Mosque, Cascade, Blue Sportsman, Bird, Veranda, Waterloo and Zebra and Elephant. Stag, Zebra and Elephant patterns were probably the series by Enoch Wood and Sons. They have a large medallion with animals and a floral border.

This nineteenth-century transfer-printed earthenware was popular before the American historical subjects. Blue pieces with American scenes by W. G. Wall and made by Andrew Stevenson were first advertised in the New York *Commercial Advertiser,* August 2, 1823. They were also made by over thirty factories and illustrated over 800 scenes in blue, pink, black, green, brown or mulberry. The deep cobalt blues were the earliest, and their designs and shapes are the best. After 1830, the lighter colors were more popular and the shapes became Victorian. An endless number of firms produced this ware, but some of the major ones specializing in the American market were Adams, Clews, Copeland, Godwin, R. Hall, J & J Jackson, T. Mayer, Meigh, Stubbs, the Ridgways and Wedgwood. English scenes were also made and are quite charming but less expensive because not so much in demand. There are castles, Italian villas and pastoral scenes with cows. Such patterns as Abbey Ruins and other Gothic patterns, and Ridgway & Co.'s Doria Stone (1844), are available at small cost. The teapots in these wares are attractive in shape, as well as in color and pattern.

Flowing Blue and Brown were also made at this time. Flowing Blue was a stone china printed with Oriental, Gothic and rustic designs. The Oriental patterns include a temple, a bamboo tree, a willow tree or a bridge. The borders are usually English in spirit. Many of the well-known potteries made Flowing Blue. Kyber and Tonquin patterns were made by William Adams. The name of the pattern was usually printed on the back of the article, and "Adams" impressed in the ware. Davenport made a pattern in Flowing Blue called Amoy, and a brown pattern called Cypress. They are marked with the impressed anchor and "Davenport." E. and J. Mayer

Leeds teapot with hand-painted chinoiserie decoration. COURTESY
MRS. ELEANOR SAWYER.

imported Arabesque, Oregon and Formosa patterns into America in the 1830's. The pieces are marked with the name of the maker and the pattern. Wedgwood's best-known Flowing Blue patterns are Knight Templar and Chapoo, an Oriental design with a flowered border. Besides the Oriental and Gothic patterns, there were flower designs such as the late Morning Glory and Shell patterns. Flowing Blue is available and comparatively inexpensive. The shape of the teapots is angular, and they are large and heavy. The value of a piece is determined by the depth and clearness of the color.

There were also gaudy wares such as Gaudy Dutch and Spatter, which were made in Staffordshire potteries for the American market. Gaudy Dutch has bold designs of flowers and leaves in deep rust red, pink, cobalt blue, apple green and lemon yellow on a frail white ground. The designs of Carnation and Grape, War Bonnet, Dove, Sunflower, Dahlia, Oyster, Urn, Zinnia and Butterfly are hand painted. Roseware is more delicate, and the patterns are King and Queen's Rose and Adam's Rose.

Spatterware is definitely country china. It was a later product. The simple sponged-on patterns include the popular and rare Peacock with green body, red tail and blue neck, marked "Adams impressed." There are also yellow, blue and red Cocks, green and red Parrots, blue, yellow and white Doves and the rare Deer. The red or blue Schoolhouse is a crude but popular pattern. Other patterns include a Star, Windmill, Cannon, Sailboat and Tulip. There are also plain spatter daubs and plaids. Spatterware is found with the names of many late Staffordshire potteries. It was also made at the American Pottery Company, Jersey City, New Jersey.

The shapes of the earliest spatterware teapots are simple

Castleford stoneware teapot with molded design and blue lines. English, early 19th century. COURTESY METROPOLITAN MUSEUM OF ART.

"Rebecca at the Well" teapot. Rockingham ware made in Ohio. COURTESY NEW YORK HISTORICAL SOCIETY.

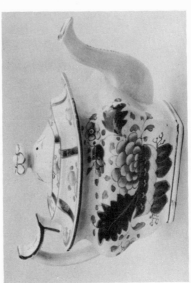

Staffordshire silver-luster teapot. Early 19th century. COURTESY METROPOLITAN MUSEUM OF ART.

"Gaudy Dutch" earthenware teapot. War Bonnet pattern. English, early 19th century. COURTESY METROPOLITAN MUSEUM OF ART.

and rounding. Later they are heavy-ridged hexagonal and octagonal sided, with heavy handles and spouts. The rarest color in spatterware is yellow, with green next. Both Gaudy Dutch and Spatter are scarce and expensive, since the demand is far beyond the supply. The old ware has the triangular kiln marks where the piece rested during the firing. This will help to distinguish the old from the reproduction where there is no maker's mark.

The Staffordshire potters also made bluish-white lead-glazed earthenware decorated in bright colors. Banded cream-ware as popular for cottages and taverns, and such ware as Mocha in patterns of checks, loops, cat's-eye and miscellaneous slip decoration, were made in teapot shapes. But jugs, bowls and mugs are easier to find.

If all of the above types of teapots are out of the range of your pocketbook, there are the Victorian wares made between 1850 and 1880. Ironstone, plain or patterned, was made in large, heavy angular teapots. Sprigged pattern in dainty green-and-pink sprigs was also made in large tea sets. Gold-band or Wedding-ring and Tea-leaf patterned china was popular in America in the late nineteenth century. These teapots are tall and low-slung and were made to hold at least a quart of tea. Gold-banded white porcelain was made in Bennington in the 1850's, and a few rare Parian tea sets with molded decoration were also made there. Flint enamel and Rockingham teapots were made in heavy ribbed designs, a rare acanthus-leaf pattern, and the popular Rebecca at the Well, which was first made at a pottery in Baltimore, but later in Ohio and elsewhere. Chelsea grape design, although a soft-paste porcelain, belongs in this category of homey Victorian ware, as does the ever-popular Willow. Both of these are still made. There are also teapots of enamelware decorated with flowers, or marbled patterns. These have metal bases, tops, handles and spouts. While not classified as antiques, these are now collectors' items but are still reasonable in price.

Pottery Cow Creamers

POTTERY COW CREAMERS were popular in England in the late eighteenth and early nineteenth centuries. These spotted cows graced the dresser of the rustic cottage and were used on festive occasions.

Pottery cow creamers are usually 6" or 7" long and from 4" to 5" high. A hole in the cow's back, with a removable cover, served to fill the jug; the curved tail was the handle, and the mouth was the spout. Whieldon made the first pottery cow creamers, following the pattern of the silver cow jugs which had been made by John Schüppe in 1755. The best-known Whieldon cows are mottled brown tortoise-shell glazed earthenware. Another Whieldon model has a milkmaid sitting beside the cow. The figures stand on a flat green base. However, there were several rare Whieldon cow jugs, examples of which are in the Katharine Prentis Murphy collection now in the New York Historical Society. One jug is mottled all over with light blue, green and light red. The eye is molded, the ears and horn are prominent, and the mouth is mooing. Another jug is black with a crisscross pattern of yellow. Beside the cow is a calf, and the figures stand on a base decorated with freehand blue circles. Other Whieldon-type jugs have large orange-yellow circles on head and cow body, and some have an allover pattern of brown and yellow spots. So varied are the mottlings and patterns that it would seem that the individual potter carried out his own whims.

Cow cream jugs were also made by many Staffordshire potters who copied the Whieldon model with the brown mottling. Some of these are mottled all over in brown; on others, the mottling is in vertical or horizontal streaks or spots of brown and tan or brown and black. Some are mottled in manganese, and a rare cow jug has a yellow glaze. The Whieldon cow creamer with the milkmaid beside the cow was also made by Staffordshire potters. Although many Staffordshire potters made cow jugs, they are not marked, so we do not know just which potteries made them. We do know that cow jugs were made by Obadiah Sherratt of Burslem (1775–1845), because of the story that he used the same mold for the Duke of Wellington's nose as for the teats of the cow. Cow jugs were also made of Pratt Ware.

A great many cow jugs were made in Wales. They were especially popular in Cornwall, and were also exported to France and Holland about 1839. Those made at the Glamorgan Works, owned by Baker, Bevans and Irwin, were decorated with freehand painting and transfer printing of black, red or green. These transfer scenes on the back and sides of the cow were of two types, with two different rustic scenes on each cow. One cow has a scene of a country house with trees on one side and on the other side two men fishing in a stream. The other scene on the printed cows had a barn with dovecote on one side and a footbridge over a stream with a man, woman and children in a boat. There are smaller prints on the lid and the stand beneath the body of the cow. Horns,

Cow creamers. Early 19th century. COURTESY GINSBURG & LEVY, INC.

Bennington cow creamer. American, mid-19th century. COURTESY METROPOLITAN MUSEUM OF ART.

ears, mouth and hoofs are black, as is the fringe of the cow's eyelashes. The bases are embossed with flowers and have a black painted band. The embossed details on figures and base vary.

Great numbers of these cow jugs were marked "Opaque China" in a scroll over the script initials "B.B.&I." Brown cows with a manganese glaze and dappled purple luster and red enamel were on a green base made on the same mold, but these are not marked. Pink luster cows were made later in the century when the firm had become Dillyn & Co. These, when marked, usually have a small impressed block capital "D." Cow milk jugs were also made at Swansea at the Cambrian Pottery (1825–1830) and of Sunderland purple-pink luster. Cambrian also made a white cow jug with painted crisscross spots of red enamel and gold on a molded green base.

Cow milk jugs were especially popular in Scotland and were made at several Scottish potteries even after 1850 when they ceased to be popular in England. North British Pottery (1810–1873) in Scotland made a cow milk jug figure of a spotted cow lying on a green base. In 1854, Don Pottery in Yorkshire made cow cream jugs with sponged decoration set on bases with bright enamel coloring. They are not marked.

In America, cow milk jugs were made at Bennington, Vermont, and in Ohio. One rare Bennington cow jug is of mottled brown "scroddle" or "agate." This ware has a laminated body and is made of rolled-out layers of different colored clay, like marble cake. Bennington also made a cow of brown mottled Rockingham and of Flint enamel in a rare light yellow and one in dark brown and blue; and graniteware cow creamers and a rare one of yellow ware. Bennington cow

Flint enamel cow creamers (1845–1885). COURTESY NEW YORK
HISTORICAL SOCIETY.

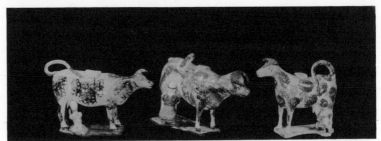

Whieldon cow creamers (1760–1780). COURTESY PHILIP SUVAL, INC.

Rockingham ware cow creamers, Bennington pottery.
COURTESY HENRY FORD MUSEUM.

creamers are $5\frac{5}{8}''$ high and $7''$ long and are on rectangular bases with rounded corners. One graniteware cow creamer in the Bennington Museum is decorated with gold and marked with the owner's name. Bennington cows can be identified by their crescent-shaped nostrils, open eyes, the folds in the neck and the visible ribs. They are not marked. The Bennington mark is the impressed stamp: "United States Pottery Company," but no cow jugs are marked, and similar wares were made by Bennington workmen at other potteries in East Liverpool, Ohio, Baltimore, Maryland, Trenton, New Jersey, after the closing of Bennington in 1858. The Rockingham cow jugs of Ohio and those made in England are usually solid brown.

The small oval lid which covers the hole on the cow's back is missing on about three-fourths of the cow jugs found today. While this may reduce the value of the jug, it does not detract from its appearance. Even these models reflect inflation prices and are expensive. Cow jugs are only found in well-established shops. Those in junk shops are usually reproductions. Many Staffordshire potters made cow cream jugs, and there are still a great number on the market, but they are in popular demand and are expensive. Since these jugs are seldom marked, they can only be identified as Staffordshire pottery.

The cows' horns differ on the various models—some are short and straight, others are longer and curved. On some cows there are scratched locks or bangs between the horns. In fact, a careful study of such details as horns or curve of tail might give a clue as to the pottery where each type of cow was made. So far, no one has attempted to classify cow creamers. A unique one is in the Gwinn collection of the

Penbrook Milk Company in Philadelphia. This was a souvenir given by the Frowd Dairy. It is marked "Sheffield Royal Dux" and bears the inscription: "Though only a cow I feel quite proud, for I bring you pure milk from the Dairy of Frowd."

Nineteenth-Century American Spoons and Souvenir Spoons

T HE EARLY American silversmiths who came from England and Holland brought with them the tools, methods and artistic traditions of the Old World, but the design of American silver is simpler and more related to its utilitarian purpose. A knowledge of historic styles is not necessary for the collector of American spoons. It is enough to know that styles in spoons, as in other silver, passed from early simplicity to ornamental.

The techniques used in silversmithing are of interest to the collector, since they help to fix the date of the piece. Early silver was raised by hammering. Later silver was spun on a lathe and casting was used. *Repoussé* and chasing were used to raise a design. In *repoussé,* the hammering is done on the underside of the article. Chasing is in lower relief, and the hammers and chisels are worked on the outside surface of the object. Engraving of designs or monograms or coats of arms was done by a sharp tool which scraped away the silver surface. The bright-cut engraving on the spoons of the late eighteenth century was done by sharp chips and gouges which gave a design of bright contrasts. Pierced designs were made by cutting holes in the silver. Sometimes designs or initials are pierced on spoon handles. Silversmiths were making spoons in America from about 1650. Their shape and method of construction changed through the years, and this helps to make the dating of spoons comparatively easy.

Early spoons were made in two pieces, the bowl and the handle. After 1800, they were made in one piece. The bowls of early spoons were wide and fig shaped. The handle was stiff, straight and short. The end of the early handle was split in two places in a shape known as trifid. For strength, the handle was fastened to the bowl of the spoon with a heavy rattail. The bowl gradually changed to an eliptical shape and then to a narrow oval. Until about 1730, the rattail was pointed and sometimes lengthened into a long V shape and decorated with an engraved design. In about 1720, the splits of the trifid handle changed to graceful curves similar to the shape of the William-and-Mary mirror top. The straight handle took a shape more comfortable to hold and the tip of the handle was bent up.

The top of the spoon handle gradually changed to a rounded arch, and the flat stem became thicker, with a ridge down the back of the stem. Then the rattail disappeared and was replaced by a rounded drop. Feather-edge and bright-cut engraving often decorated the spoon handles. The next development in the handle end was the coffin shape about 1800. It was an American innovation. By 1815, these handles were decorated with the popular shell, sheaf-of-wheat or basket-of-flowers decoration. Many families have spoons of this type with fiddle-shaped handles and decorative handle ends. They were often made by local silversmiths. By 1830, the raised designs on the handles were stamped and cast and

Teaspoons, fine-cut pattern made by Benjamin Halstead, New York c. 1780–1790. COURTESY METROPOLITAN MUSEUM OF ART.

Teaspoon with "coffin handle," made by C. D. Sullivan & Co., St. Louis, Mo., early 19th century. COURTESY METROPOLITAN MUSEUM OF ART.

Teaspoons with sheaf-of-wheat design made by Patrick Martin, Philadelphia, 1825. COURTESY METROPOLITAN MUSEUM OF ART.

were more elaborate, sometimes covering the whole handle of the spoon; by the middle of the century, spoons were heavy and ornately decorated in high relief.

American silver spoons are usually marked with a stamp of the maker's name or initials within a depressed rectangle, shield, oval or heart. Sometimes the name of the city or town was added. By 1830, spoons were often marked with the name of the seller rather than the maker. American silver has no hallmarks, but such marks as Coin, Pure Coin, Standard, Dollar, Premium or C or D were used to designate the standard of the silver. The word Sterling did not come into general use until after 1860. American spoons are not as plentiful as English spoons, and the collector today cannot hope to find one with the mark of a seventeenth- or eighteenth-century American maker. These pieces are in museums.

But the path for collecting nineteenth-century American spoons is open for the collector. There are few spoons before 1825 available, but occasionally one runs across a spoon with delicate, bright-cut engraving in an Adam swag design on its oval-ended handle. The thin spoons with plain fiddle-shaped handle are engraved with script initials and stamped with the name of maker or seller. These were often decorated with a stamped or cast sheaf-of-wheat, basket-of-flowers or thread design with a shell. Because these spoons have not been considered important up to now, they are still procurable at reasonable prices. The silver spoons of the mid- and late nineteenth century, with designs that were stamped or cast and almost covered the handles, and the heavy ornate pieces decorated in high relief made after 1860 and spurned a few years ago, are now also of interest to the collector. They are all sterling silver, and the workmanship and designs are excellent in many cases. The bright-cut engraved and chased designs in patterns such as the rose, lily, star, honeysuckle, wheat or rosette, are marked "Sterling," with the company's name and patent date usually in the 1880's or 1890's. Other designs such as Persian, Egyptian, Italian or Japanese were more ornate and heavier. Embossed and cast designs had cameos, animal heads and figures. These are the antiques of tomorrow.

The souvenir spoons of late Victorian days are already a popular field for the collector. The interest here is historical. Both social and patriotic American history is recorded on them. Places, events, people, legends and tales long forgotten are brought to light and preserved in picture and story. These spoons are usually made of heavy sterling silver, and in many cases the designs are excellent.

The fashion of collecting souvenir spoons came from abroad. Galt of Washington, D. C. made the first American souvenir spoon—an embossed head of Washington on the handle. Daniel Low of Salem is also credited with introducing the souvenir spoon to America with his famous Salem Witch spoons. That with the witch and cat figures is the most interesting, although the simpler pattern was made first. Daniel Low also made a spoon with Hawthorne's head, a figure of Leif Ericson and a Lexington and Concord spoon. In 1890–1891, a booklet, "Souvenir Spoons of America," was published by the Jewelers Circular Publishing Company, 189 Broadway, New York. It gives a list of spoons with maker's names and descriptions, as well as pictures of the souvenir spoons made in America up to that date. A book on American souvenir spoons was published by George B. James, Jr. in 1890, which also lists and describes the earliest

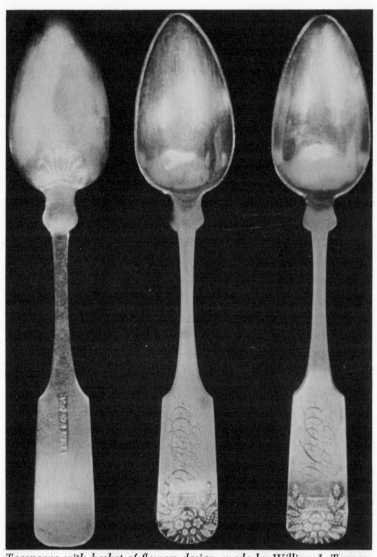

*Teaspoons with basket-of-flowers design, made by William I. Tenney,
New York City, 1840.* COURTESY NEW YORK HISTORICAL SOCIETY.

types. Some of the most interesting, from the design stand-point, were manufactured by the Gorham Manufacturing Company in 1890. It patterned its spoons after the fashion-able European souvenir spoons. A group of Nürnberg spoons had handles with silhouette figures of German peasants, burghers and nobles. A group called "Old Paris" included twelve coffee spoons with designs of figures of a ship, armored knight, cupid and other subjects from old French prints. The crests of various nations formed another series. Then the company put out Evangelist spoons to be given for christen-ings. Those with American scenes made at this time included Washington Irving with a picture of Sunnyside; three with scenes of Detroit, Michigan; spoons of Cambridge, Massachu-setts, Rochester, New York, Louisville, Kentucky, Pittsburgh, Pennsylvania, Baltimore, Maryland and other American cities. The most interesting are the spoons of Brooklyn and New York with the profile of the Statue of Liberty; of Gettys-burg, with the silhouettes of Victory and General Meade; and of Saratoga, with the Indian silhouette. Penn's Treaty spoon, with Independence Hall and the Liberty Bell, is also a popular one.

One interesting collection included eagles and Indians; another would be assembled of scenes such as Niagara Falls, Charter Oak, the Maine pine tree. National monuments form another group; cities and local history included the Chicago Fire; emblems of states were still another. Poets and writers such as Whittier, Hawthorne and Longfellow offer another group. The Actor's Fund spoon of 1892 is also in demand. Then there are spoons of expositions and world's fairs from the Columbian Exposition of 1893 to both New York World's Fairs. Resort hotels long since destroyed are shown on some

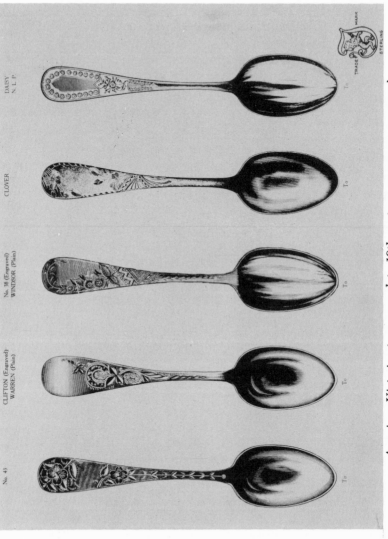

American Victorian teaspoons, late 19th century. COURTESY JEWELER'S
CIRCULAR KEYSTONE.

Silver souvenir spoons, c. 1890–1900. Top row, left to right: 1) St. James Cathedral, Montreal, on gold-washed bowl, beaver handle. Marks: Birks/Sterling. 2) Statue of Liberty on terminal; Brooklyn Bridge in relief on bowl. Marks of Gorham Manufacturing Co./Sterling. 3) Indian on terminal; colonists' landing scene in relief on bowl. Marks: Bigelow-Kennard & Co./Sterling; and marks of Gorham Manufacturing Co. 4) Maid carrying chocolate tray on terminal; bowl inscribed "Walter Baker & Co. Limited / Dorchester / Mass. / Breakfast Cocoa"; no marks. 5) Indian handle; buffalo in bowl. Mark unidentified (H on pennant). Sterling. Bottom row, left to right: 1) William Penn on terminal. In gold-washed bowl, Philadelphia City Hall. Marks: J. E. Caldwell & Co. / Sterling. 2) Eagle and sunrise on terminal. In relief on bowl, Fort Dearborn, Chicago. Marks: Hyman Berg & Co./Sterling. 3) General Ulysses Grant on terminal; rifle on shank; Grant's log cabin on bowl. Souvenir of 1904 World's Fair, St. Louis. No marks. Silver-plated. 4) Prospector's mule on terminal; scene of Royal Gorge in bowl. Mark unidentified (H in circle). Sterling. 5) Cutout scene of Salt Lake City on terminal; spoon shovel-shaped, of polished copper. Marks unidentified (crown, W, anchor). PHOTOGRAPH COURTESY OF THE SMITHSONIAN INSTITUTION.

of these memory spoons, and an early locomotive tops the list of those representing American industries. Silhouette handles range from the Witch of Salem, Uncle Sam, the Totem Pole in the Museum of Natural History to a salmon of the Columbia River in Oregon or the cactus of Prescott, Arizona. There is also a category of California spoons including the miner of '49, the California Bear, the San Francisco Fire, Coronado, San Diego and Point Loma. The majority of these were manufactured by Shreve & Company, the best-known jewelers of San Francisco. The most sought-after souvenir spoons are those with silhouettes of figures on the stems. Other collectors look for spoons with cutout silhouettes of cities, such as that of the San Francisco Fire of 1906.

Although souvenir spoons represent one of the most popular collecting fields in America today, there are many on the market, and the prices—although they have risen in the last few years—are still reasonable. The average collector is more interested in subject matter and story than in workmanship or design. The collecting of old silver spoons even of late vintage can be satisfying because of the beauty of the material itself and the artistry of the object. In the past, a silver collection required time and care, but with the new long-lasting cleaners and polishes much of the chore of owning silver is removed. Spoons thus cleaned, mounted on a dark background, and framed in airtight glass-covered frames will stay clean for years.

This chapter has given some of the history of spoons and the possibilities for the collector today. There are many books which give the collector details of souvenir spoons.

Viands in Pottery and Porcelain

GAME, FRUIT AND VEGETABLES IN POTTERY AND PORCELAIN

THE IDEA for tureens and other pottery in animal and vegetable forms came—as so many influences in ceramics—direct from China. There were brilliantly colored Chinese porcelain duck tureens, and apples, quince, figs and other fruits and vegetables were also made in Chinese pottery and porcelain. European pottery copied these forms in the dinnerware of the eighteenth century.

Until the eighteenth century, food itself was the only attraction on the dinner table, but then the dining room came into its own. Tablecloths of velvet, silk damask and brocade set off the services of sterling silver. Large epergnes and centerpieces of silver and porcelain were designed to hold fruit, sweets and flowers. Serving dishes were made in the shapes of colorful and decorative food. Sugared flummeries in the form of Solomon's temple, moonshine and fish ponds, and dessert frames of garden scenes enhanced the dessert course. Amid these pleasurable surroundings the gourmet thrived.

Rouen pottery pieces made in the forms of birds and animals, dressed as they were served at the table, date from the early eighteenth century. Tureens were made in the form of pheasants, hares and ducks, and there were also tureens with groups of dead game on their covers, and plates with fruit in relief. Rouen faience is thick and heavy and is decorated in blue and polychrome. A similar faience was also made at Strasbourg from the beginning of the eighteenth century and was copied in Marseilles. A covered dish with polychrome decoration and dead ducks on the cover, a tureen in the shape of a pigeon, and a naturalistic melon tureen on a plate decorated with flowers, were also made in Strasbourg. A large hen-and-chickens tureen was made at Sceaux. A pair of tureens in the shape of quail were made at Le Moustiers in the Ferrat pottery between 1760 and 1789. They are polychrome with blue, brown, yellow, green and violet colorings.

However, the French, who get most of the credit for delicacies of the table, were not the only ones to eat among decorative surroundings. Pottery viands were particularly popular in Germany and were made of almost all regional potteries. As early as the seventeenth century, enameled pottery table services were made in the form of animals and vegetables at Schretzheim, Germany. Among the pieces were ham, boars' heads and melon-shaped tureens.

Naturalistic blue fish were made at Fürstenburg and Nürnberg. A hen-and-chickens tureen comes from Proscau, and a grape tureen from Frankfurt. There were also duck, swan and turkey tureens of German Frankenthal pottery. Two squash on a plate were made at Göggingen, and cauliflower and asparagus standing upright on a plate was an early piece made at Bayreuth. Cauliflower and asparagus dishes were also made at Amberg, Augsburg and Strasbourg.

Pigeons, ducks and other birds were popular for covered

Pigeon tureen. Strasbourg, 18th century. COURTESY
METROPOLITAN MUSEUM OF ART.

*Pair of dishes in form of birds in nests. Moustiers,
Ferrat, mid-19th century.* COURTESY METROPOLITAN
MUSEUM OF ART.

*Sauce boat with fox head and swan handle. English
lead-glazed earthenware, late 18th century.* COURTESY
METROPOLITAN MUSEUM OF ART.

dishes. A beautiful brown, white and yellow pigeon comes from Friedberg, a dove from Mosbach, and eggs in a basket of Durlach pottery. A black-and-white duck with yellow bill and feet comes from Künersburg. A boar's-head covered dish was made at Höchst, and a yellow-and-gray pig with an acorn branch was made at Braunschweig. In the mideighteenth century, at least one pottery in Brussels, Belgium, was manufacturing faience in the form of plates of asparagus, oval and round tureens in the shape of cabbages, melons, artichokes, pigeons, cocks, turkeys, eels and baskets of fruit.

The decoration and coloring were excellent and even considered superior to similar articles made at Delft and Rouen. A small red-and-green artichoke tureen has delicate line decoration, and pair of gorgeous blue-green melon tureens decorated with a molded yellow-green vine and leaves show the excellence of Brussels faience. The cabbage, cauliflower and lettuce tureens were especially popular in continental potteries. There are green and red cabbages and several types of lettuce, including romaine. Asparagus tureens of various sizes are bound with decorative blue or pink ribbons. There were also pottery artichokes, squash, pumpkins and cucumbers, as well as tureens in the shapes of apples, pears, pineapples, pomegranates, lemons, figs and grapes. These shapes were made in many other continental potteries including those in Holland, Switzerland, Norway, Sweden, Italy and Spain.

In 1753, a factory for the manufacture of faience was established in Copenhagen, Denmark, and tureens were made in the forms of geese, cocks and animals. Similar faience with a stanniferous enamel was made in Norway, Sweden, Portugal, Spain and Italy. A large Italian fish tureen of pinkish-cream color has a lemon and leaves as an appropriate finial. Fish tureens are also typical of Portugal and Spain. One of the most characteristic pieces of Spanish pottery is a plate with green and red peppers. There are also plates with molded walnuts and almonds.

In Delft faience there are attractive duck tureens of several sizes. The bottom of the tureen is often a nest on which the duck sits. There are also rabbit tureens of various sizes, and fruits such as melons, apples, lemons, grapes and nuts with removable lids. English potteries as early as Whieldon made green glazed teapots, coffeepots and other dishes with naturalistic molded shapes of cauliflowers and pineapples. Whieldon also made dove tureens. The mauve and gray doves sat on russet nestlike dishes. A green-and-brown glazed fox-and-geese sauceboat was made in the mideighteenth century, and plates were made in green glaze leaf shapes.

In seventeenth- and eighteenth-century still-life paintings, the game pie is often depicted. There is the famous "Swan Pie" of Heda, and the "Dead Wolf" of Oudry, with the crust of the pie partly eaten. In another picture, the game-pie dish is broken open, revealing two whole rabbits inside. Rabbit pie was a favorite dish in old cookery books, and it was the custom to serve it in a crust. When the Napoleonic Wars brought on a shortage of flour in the early 1800's Wedgwood made game-pie dishes in *en croûte* designs, to imitate the flour pastry. These were decorated with molded patterns of game—rabbits, ducks or geese. Some were also made with lattice tops on round shapes for serving pies and small tarts. Pie dishes with crisscross crusts were also made in Lucerne, Switzerland, in the eighteenth century, and melon, grape, pear and cabbage tureens were made at Lucerne and at Winterthur potteries.

Wedgwood made cane-body dishes ornamented with white

jasper, to imitate iced cakes. Wedgwood dishes in the shapes of leaves, which were used as pickle and sardine dishes, were made in fish shapes. The idea of leaves as pickle dishes also came from the Chinese, but they were made in all English potteries including salt-glaze Whieldon ware, Worcester, Chelsea, Bow, Longton Hall, Lowestoft porcelain and Staffordshire potteries. A Wedgwood confiture dish is made in green glaze in the shape of a bunch of grapes. Wedgwood also made dishes in the shape of pineapples, artichokes, scallops and other shells, as well as melon-shaped tureens and beehive butter tubs. Later nineteenth-century vegetables and fruit forms were made in Majolica.

The melon-shape tureen is one of the most popular of all pottery food forms. It had been made in many continental potteries and was fashioned of English creamware at Leeds, Longton Hall and other potteries, as well as at Wedgwood. Some melon tureens are cream color; others are in realistic melon colorings. These are usually set on a decorative plate. A rare quail tureen was made at Worcester, and quail tureens were also made of Lowestoft pottery. Staffordshire covered dishes included brown, green and yellow naturalistic-looking ducks sitting on pottery dishes in a soft blue.

However, the most elaborate and decorative dishes in the shape of foods were the porcelains made at Meissen and Chelsea in the eighteenth century. Meissen served as the model. There were duck, swan, hen-and-chicken tureens, and there were also smaller Meissen porcelain models in the shape of apples, lemons and melons. Meissen dessert dishes were made in the form of artichokes. These were realistic in outline, but imaginative in color; they had added decorative detail such as finials in the shape of birds, snails, caterpillars or vines.

Melon tureen, Leeds pottery, 18th century. COURTESY VICTORIA AND ALBERT MUSEUM, LONDON.

Hen-and-chicken tureen. Chelsea, 18th century. COURTESY VICTORIA AND ALBERT MUSEUM, LONDON.

Rabbit tureen, Chelsea porcelain, 18th century. COURTESY VICTORIA AND ALBERT MUSEUM, LONDON.

The English porcelain factories at Bristol, Bow, Derby and Chelsea made similar shapes between 1750 and 1770, but Chelsea excelled in both quantity and quality. There were Chelsea porcelain tureens in the shape of melons, pineapples, asparagus, lettuce, cauliflowers, artichokes and cabbages. There was also the amusing Chelsea tiny pea-in-the-pod. There were small fruit tureens in the shape of figs, grapes, pears, lemons and pomegranates, and the popular melon and small pineapple-shaped dessert dishes. But the *chef-d'oeuvre* of Chealsea porcelain were the elaborate tureens in the shapes of rabbits, pigeons, ducks, swans, boars' heads or hen-and-chickens.

Some of these continued to be made in the nineteenth century, but while the forms of the fruit or vegetable are realistic, the decoration is simpler. Both Wedgwood and Staffordshire potteries made green glaze pineapple and grape tureens. Luster apples were made of Staffordshire pottery, while Wedgwood made shell tureens in moonlight luster. All of these dishes are rare and expensive but so beautiful in color, design and workmanship that even one piece would enhance a sideboard. Don't expect to start with a Chelsea pea-in-the-pod, for they are every inch an aristocrat and extremely rare and expensive.

VI

Victoriana

Staffordshire figure of Queen Victoria made in 1887, to celebrate the Year of Jubilee. COURTESY SMITHSONIAN INSTITUTION.

Victorian Cardcases and
Calling Cards

———

A CARDCASE for calling cards was an essential part of the
polite ceremony of Victorian visiting. These cases were
often beautiful in material and workmanship. They were
made of gold or silver, engraved and even set with semiprecious stones or small enamel medallions. They were also
made of ivory carved in China, mother-of-pearl, carved or
inlaid silver filigree, piqué and tortoise shell. Piqué cutout
designs in gold and silver were first made in Italy. They became popular in Paris and England in the eighteenth century, and in 1872, they were machine made in Birmingham,
England.

Perhaps the most popular Victorian cardcase was that made
of mother-of-pearl. The mother-of-pearl was cut in small
squares, diamonds and circles and arranged in various all-over
patterns of both light and smoky mother-of-pearl. Sometimes
there was a carved central plaque or a silver cartouche with
a monogram or a flower spray of roses or lilies of the valley.
Sometimes the mother-of-pearl was carved or engraved or
silver inlaid with small sprays of flowers or birds. Carved

plaques of engraved mother-of-pearl were also framed in tortoise shell. Papier-mâché cardcases had medallions of mother-of-pearl.

Some cardcases were made of beadwork or mosaic. The mosaic cases were probably brought as souvenirs from Italy. There were also cases of silver or Sheffield plate made with stamped architectural scenes of St. Paul's Cathedral, Westminster Abbey or the Houses of Parliament, as souvenirs of visits to these places. These thin rectangular cardcases had a top which lifted off and revealed a narrow slit just large enough to hold about a half-dozen cards. Cardcases must have been in use in the eighteenth century too, for while there are no advertisements offering them for sale in America then, Thomas Coram, Engraver, advertised in the Charleston *Royal Gazette* October 24, 1781: "Visiting and compliment cards engraved and printed." While the name on the formal visiting card was probably always engraved on a white card, the same Thomas Coram advertised in the *Carolina and American Gazette,* January 28, 1779: "A few packs of visiting cards in the present taste and neatly printed in purple and other colors."

By the middle of the nineteenth century, visiting cards became more decorative and sentimental. At first they were covered with beautiful embossing of flowers or scenes, and in the case of a widow or widower, with a scene of a gravestone sheltered by a weeping willow. Cards were also hand painted and written by professional penmen. For a very small sum, the customer could have a package of visiting cards with flourishes and birds or flowers and a name or an inscription. Card writing was an itinerant trade. The writers usually worked on street corners at small folding desks. They special-

Victorian cardcases. Top row: silver with embossed St. Paul's Cathedral, mother-of-pearl Chinese design, diamond pattern, silver, Westminster Abbey. Lower row: tortoise shell with silver name plate, tortoise shell inlaid with mother-of-pearl, ivory with carved medallion, carved tortoise shell with light tortoise border. COURTESY NEW YORK HISTORICAL SOCIETY.

ized in writing visiting cards, and their work had the appearance of copperplate printing.

In less fastidious circles, cards were decorated with the new chromolithography. Favorite designs included floral wreaths, moss roses, lilies of the valley, turtledoves and pigeons. Cards imported by Alling Brothers, Northford, Connecticut, included chromo and beveled edges. The Dempsey and Carroll catalogue of 1880 listed chromo cards: "Pack of 50—no two alike, 10¢ . . . Hand and Floral, 2 for 35¢, Paris Beauties."

In about 1860, German decalcomania also became popular. These thin cardboard motifs of flowers and birds, wreaths, baskets and hands holding a spray of flowers could be bought in sheets, and My Lady could paste one of these sentimental bits over her name on her calling card.

Some cards also had featherwork birds as corner decoration. In the Landauer Collection, an agent's sample book of S. M. Foote, Northford, Connecticut, gives a picture of the various types of calling cards of the late nineteenth century. In addition to the chromo cards with hands and sprays, there were plain cards with gold edges and a turned-down corner or fancy cut corners. Others had embossed baskets, wreaths or horseshoes, and some were fan or slipper shaped. There were navy-blue or cardinal-red cards with gold printing, and cards with a gold border or a black border for mourning. Some were printed on various colored marble papers such as "gold granite snowflake, Scotch marble and transparent," and other backgrounds were covered with printed designs such as Gothic, Oriental, Persian or morning glory.

Still other cards could be had with sentimental phrases: "Remember Me," "I live on love for thee," "Forever Yours," "Forget Me Not" or "Believe me True." It was also the

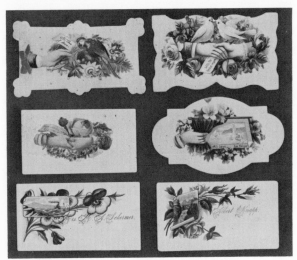

American calling cards. Second half 19th century.
COURTESY NEW YORK HISTORICAL SOCIETY.

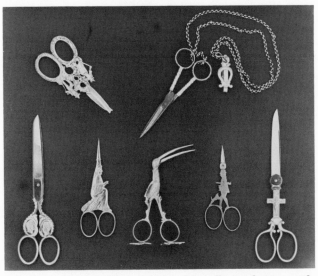

Top left: Scissors, plain blades, foliated handles and grips with rustic figures of man and woman above finger holes. Top right: Scissors with silver handles, chain and belt clip. Marks on clip unidentified. Bottom, left to right: 1) Scissors with gold-washed handles and grips. Inset medallions of King George V and Queen Mary. Blades marked: "A. Schnittert / Solingen." 2) Scissors with gold-washed handles in shape of witch on broomstick. Handle marked: "Salem 1692 / Registered / Germany." 4) Metal scissors; figure of hunter and dog on handles. 5) Scissors with gold-washed handles with crucifix.

fashion to have one's photograph printed on one side of the card.

There are many of these nineteenth-century cards available today. They may be found pasted in old scrapbooks or loose in boxes of old letters, valentines or other paper tokens. I found mine in an old barn shop by a roadside in Vermont. However, the old decalcomanias are available and some dealers are using these to make up cards.

Perhaps the only way to distinguish the old from the new is the condition of the card. The old ones are yellow with age and seldom in perfect condition. There are collections of ornamental nineteenth-century calling cards in museums, libraries and historical societies throughout the country. In the collection at the New York Public Library is a small card which belonged to Tom Thumb. It is 1¼" by ⅝" and printed: "Gen. Tom Thumb." A collection of these colorful sentimental cards could be mounted on a colored background and framed. Six or eight cards together would be attractive, and several of these group mountings could be hung together on a wall.

Victorian Scissors, Thimbles and Sewing Birds

———

QUEEN VICTORIA set the fashion for needlework, and in the middle and late nineteenth century, it was considered the most elegant of female accomplishments. Following Victoria's example, as recorded in her childhood diary, young children were taught to make needlebooks and pincushions. Then there was the cross-stitch sampler which was devised not only to teach stitches but to give moral instruction. There were also tatting, embroidering, Berlin work and quiltmaking. All these industries of the Victorian needlewoman required needles, emeries to keep them in condition, needlecases, thimbles, scissors, spool racks and vises or sewing birds to keep the work in place.

To store these fascinating accessories of needlework, there were small necessaries which held scissors, needles, bodkin and thimble, but there were also sewing baskets, and for the more affluent, French workboxes of polished wood or papier-mâché inlaid with metal or mother-of-pearl, and boxes of quillwork or inlaid Tunbridge Ware. A velvet-covered shelf in the top of the box had fitted spaces for scissors, needlecase, thimble, thread and bodkin.

A present of such a workbox from Paris or an ivory carved or lacquered box from China was the most prized of all gifts. These workboxes and their contents have become collectors' items today. Some collectors include the whole subject of needlework, but others specialize in thimbles, sewing birds or expensive etuis. Indeed, there are many fascinating antiques in the sewing box. Even emery fruits, although limited, can be interesting, for there are not only red strawberries but grapes, pears, peaches and pomegranates, with or without silver tops. Darning eggs were made in carved or painted wood, some with transfer-printed souvenir scenes.

There are also ivory-turned darning eggs and eggs made of semiprecious stones such as quartz, marble and malachite. Needlecases were made of wood, ivory, mother-of-pearl, horn, straw, silver or gold. They were sometimes covered with materials such as Scotch plaid, velvet, brocade or beading. There are also fascinating European carved wooden figures of peasants, Orientals, Napoleon and the American Darby and Joan.

Scissors developed from primitive shears which were made centuries before Christ in Egypt, Greece, Rome and other parts of the world. By the sixteenth century, shears had developed into long-bladed scissors of ornamented steel, and by the seventeenth century, there were iron scissors with round points and pierced and chiseled decoration, and small embroidery scissors with shanks the shape of a woman's legs, with fancy boots. These *"Jambes des Princesses"* were popular in France and are of a type still made today.

Other embroidery scissors were pierced, engraved or inlaid with silver or gold designs. In the eighteenth century, small and dainty embroidery scissors, $2\frac{1}{2}''$ to $3\frac{1}{2}''$ long, in decora-

Woman with sewing box, c. 1845. COURTESY ABBY ROCKEFELLER, FOLK ART COLLECTION, WILLIAMSBURG, VA.

tive cases, were given as engagement presents along with verses praising the virtues of fidelity and love. Scissors with the names cut in metal were made by Rogers & Sons, Sheffield, England, in the midnineteenth century. The stock names used were: Amelia, Anne, Abbey, Clarissa, Emily, Eliza, Harriet, Julia, Lois, Martha and Maria.

The Art Union July 1845, illustrates scissors with scrolls and the cutout name "Victoria." These were made by Mr. Prior and Mr. Peach and were exhibited at the Paris Exposition. Rudd and Wainwright are mentioned as exhibiting scissors with an "admirable likeness" of Cobden and Bright cut in the solid steel. (Cobden and Bright were radical members of Parliament during Victoria's reign.) *The Art Union,* January 1846, describes the skill and workmanship of scissors with swans, dragons and butterflies in the handles. These were made by Thomas Wilkinson and Son of Sheffield, who also made a pair of scissors which was presented to Queen Victoria. The decoration included the British Coat of Arms and the name Victoria in cutout letters and "is considered to be the most perfect specimen of steel ever produced in Sheffield."

"Scissors of a bird form, the beaks making the blades" were made by Rogers and Company, who also made scissors with dolphins, fish and scrolls on the handles. The Hobson Company showed five or six thousand designs "known by quaint and peculiar names" in its pattern books. In the display of the City of Sheffield, England, at the exhibition of 1851, there were many different designs of ornamental scissors. Some had cutout ivory or bone handles; others were of delicate enamel. Damascened decorated scissors were made in Toledo, Spain.

There was a thimble factory in England as early as 1696, and undoubtedly thimbles reached America at this time, in addition to the few that may have been brought over by Pilgrim needlewomen. There is no record of early American silversmiths making thimbles, and the newspaper ads of the eighteenth century indicate that they were imported from England. The first ad mentioning thimbles is that of Thomas Brown, Cutler, at the Sign of the Cross Daggers near the Fly Market—"Sells all sorts of Ironmongery and cutlery Ware . . . Thimbles, Pins, and Needles . . ."—in the New York *Weekly Post-Boy,* May 19, 1746. Benjamin Halsted, who had been a gold- and silversmith in New York for some years, advertised "a few best steel top thimbles" in the New York *Gazette or Weekly Post-Boy,* September 25, 1766. Silver thimbles with steel tops and silver tops continued to be advertised in New York and Philadelphia newspapers through 1785, but the ads all indicate that the thimbles were imported. However Paul Revere made a gold thimble for his wife.

From careful research of newspaper ads of the eighteenth century, we come to the conclusion that the first thimbles made in any quantity in America were of ivory, not silver. Charles Shipman, Ivory and Hardwood Turner of Birmingham, England, advertised "ivory thimbles" and "eggs" among a long list of turners' articles in the New York *Journal for the General Advertiser* August 6, 1767.

The first thimble manufactory in America was run by the silversmith Benjamin Halsted, who had been in business in New York and Elizabeth Town, New Jersey, since 1764, according to newspaper notices. The ad, which is worth quoting because it gives a picture of early American industry, appeared in the *Diary or Evening Register* August 10, 1794:

Benjamin Halstead—Thimble Manufactory. Benjamin Halstead respectfully informs his Friends and the Public in general, that he still continues carrying on the gold and silversmith business No. 67 Broad Street; he has brought the manufactory of gold, silver and Pinchbeck Thimbles with steel top to great perfection and thinks he could make a sufficient quantity to supply the United States Citizens, consider your interest, and encourage American Manufactures.

Those imported are of the Slightest kind, I will engage that one of mine, will do more service than 3 of them, and I know by experience, that imported ones of the quality of mine cost 18 shillings per doz. and could not be sold by 25 percent, as low as mine. Every dealer in this article will soon find the advantage of keeping Halsted's Thimbles and have the satisfaction of knowing that he does his customers justice. Silver and steel Bodkins, tooth and ear picks by the doz. or single.

By the first quarter of the nineteenth century, a few New York silversmiths were listed as "thimble makers." The following ad, showing a workman at his bench, appeared in the Philadelphia *Directory* of 1824: "James Peters, gold and silver thimble and Pencil Case Manufacturer." At about this same time, according to Elizabeth Galbraith Sickels in the *Antiques Journal*, September 1964, David Platt, who had been making thimbles in Huntington, Long Island, moved to New York; and in the New York *Directory* of 1824–1825, Potter and Platt, thimble manufacturers, were at 361 Pearl Street. Platt continued in business until 1842 when he retired, but the firm went on into the twentieth century. There is a gold thimble decorated with red-gold flowers and green leaves and engraved "S. Platt" in the Huntington Historical Society. It was made by David Platt in 1828, for his wife.

In 1826, George Pratt took Ezra Conklin Prime as an apprentice, and Prime later established a thimble manufactory at Huntington, Long Island, which continued in the Prime family and manufactured thimbles until 1890. A thimble made at this factory is also at the Huntington Historical Society.

Thimbles were made of many different materials. There were metal thimbles of gold, silver, brass, steel, iron and pinchbeck (a combination of copper and zinc invented in 1732 to imitate gold), wood, hard rubber and plastic. The decoration on metal thimbles includes chasing, embossing, engraving, enameling, damascene, niello and raised and cut-out designs. Many eighteenth-century thimbles had steel or carnelian tops, and sometimes amethysts, moonstones or other semiprecious stones were used. Gold and silver thimbles usually had a band with an engraved monogram or a chased or embossed design, or the band was set with stones. Chinese thimbles were often carved from pearls and had bands of engraved gold. There were also thimbles made of silver filigree.

Glass, porcelain and enamel thimbles were the most colorful and decorative. Thimbles of Venetian glass were decorated with flowers and leaves in opaque and clear glass. English enamel thimbles were painted with quaint landscape scenes and the tops are gilded copper. There are also pink Battersea enamel thimbles. Porcelain thimbles were made in the eighteenth century of Dresden porcelain, and in England at Chelsea, Derby and of Royal Worcester porcelain. These were usually of white porcelain with flower-and-leaf decoration in color and gold. Some thimbles were made with enamel bands showing windmills and other Dutch scenes. Victorian

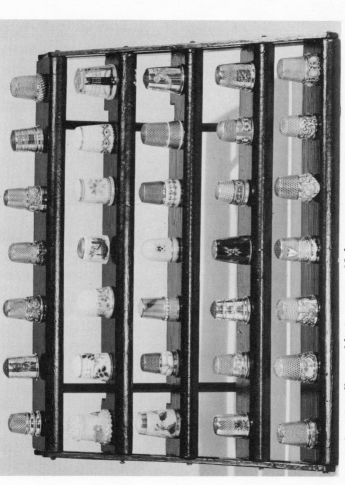

Top shelf, left to right: 1) Yellow gold. American, 19th century. 2) Yellow gold with carnelian set in apex, handmade. Swedish, c. 1771. 3) Yellow gold with chased band having applied green-gold design and rim, four flowers set with turquoise. English, 18th century. 4) Yellow gold with black-enamel design. American, 19th century. 5) Yellow gold with red, yellow and white gold flowers and green-gold leaves applied on a chased band. A plain oval on band is engraved with the initials "M.M." and a like oval on the opposite side is engraved with a coronet. French (Paris marks), 19th century. 6) Yellow gold with silver-colored metal set in apex, handmade. Continental, 18th century. 7) Red gold with yellow-gold band, "Feb. 28, 1891" engraved inside. American.

Second shelf, left to right: 1) Opaline with three pink clear-glass flowers with yellow opaque-glass centers and green clear-glass leaves applied to side. White and yellow opaque glass applied to edge. Venetian, 18th century. 2) White porcelain (Derby) with emerald-green leaves outlined in gold, and all other decorations in gold. English, 18th century. 3) White porcelain (Dresden) with light-blue flowers, and all other decorations in gold. Only the band is glazed. German, 18th century. 4) English enamel. The scene is enclosed in a raised yellow scroll frame. The body of the thimble is white enamel inside and out over a copper base. Gilded apex. 18th century. 5) White porcelain (Chelsea) with large pink and small blue flowers and green leaves, gold bands. English, 18th century. 6) White porcelain (Derby) with cobalt-blue enamel ribbon and dots and all other decorations in gold. English, 19th century. 7) Glass. American, 20th century.

Third shelf, left to right: 1) Sterling, gilded inside, light-blue enamel background with pink flowers and green leaves, moonstone set in apex. Continental, 19th century. 2) Silver-gilded inside, Delft band. Continental, Holland, 19th century. 3) Sterling gilt with robin's-egg-blue enamel band in which a raised thread of gold makes a design, small white opaque stones set above band, moonstone set in apex. German, 19th century. 4) Mother-of-pearl with two pinchbeck bands, enameled pansy medallion inlaid on side. French, 18th century. 5) Silver, gilded inside, light-blue enamel band with pink roses and green leaves, carnelian set in apex. Continental, 19th century. 6) Sterling gilt with green enamel band enclosed by two narrow white opaque enamel bands. French (Paris marks), 20th century. 7) Silver, gilded inside, amethyst set in apex. Danish.

Fourth shelf, left to right: 1) Gold-plated brass. American, patented 1859. 2) Gold-plated sterling silver with applied design of a woman swimming. American, 20th century. 3) Gold-plated silver. Design is cut through gold showing silver, carnelian set in apex. Continental, 19th century. 4) Tortoise shell laid over silver with gold top and three inlaid gold designs on side, 19th century. 5) Gold-plated base metal with overlaid band of Damascene work on Toledo steel. Spanish, 20th century. 6) Gold-plated sterling silver with lilies-of-the-valley and bowknot design. American, 20th century. 7) Gold-plated copper. American, 19th century.

Bottom shelf, left to right: 1) Silver, gilded inside, set with turquoise. Italian, 19th century. 2) Silver with gold band. Hand-cut design on chased ground. American, 19th century. 3) Sterling with gold band, wild-rose design. American, 20th century. 4) Silver with scalloped edge, carnelian set in apex, gilded inside. Continental, 19th century. 5) Sterling with gold band, one large wild rose elongating band. American, 20th century. 6) Sterling with gold band, raised scroll design. American, 19th century. 7) Silver, gilded applied pierced band set with opals. Italian, c. 1900. FROM THE COLLECTION OF ELIZABETH GALBRAITH SICKELS. PHOTO BY MAC BALL STUDIO.

thimbles were decorated with mother-of-pearl and tortoise shell overlaid with silver in a design of pansies and bands of gold. Gold and silver thimbles manufactured by Ketcham and McDougall of New York in the late nineteenth and twentieth centuries were decorated with chased and embossed designs. Patterns included the embossed scroll, embroidery allover, allover embossed and Louis XV.

Some thimbles had engraved borders with lily of the valley, wild rose and daisy. Others had bands of bird and landscape, two men on bicycles, house and landscape, a dog's head or a chased scroll with an eagle. There were thimbles with plain fluted borders and rope bands. Some had appliqué colored flowers enameled and gilded. Simons Brothers made gold and silver thimbles in the late nineteenth century, and the designs on their gold thimbles included a chased ivory border, a Dutch windmill, a lighthouse and ship, a sailing boat, a bird and a strap and buckle. They also made silver thimbles with designs of a house and tree and flower and butterfly, as well as more simple patterns.

One of the interesting categories of thimble collecting is the souvenir field. There are thimbles with Easter lilies from Bermuda and thistles from Scotland, and porcelain thimbles with birds and flowers were made as souvenirs from Oxford, Exeter and Chester. Some others have scenes of England, including the Thames and London Bridge. Historic thimbles include a World War Liberty Bell engraved: "Proclaim liberty in the land to the inhabitants—by order of the Assembly of Pennsylvania in Philadelphia, 1752," made by Simons Brothers of Philadelphia.

Other World's Fair thimbles were: Chicago World's Fair, 1892; "1492 World's Columbian Exposition, 1892"; "1492

World's Columbian Exposition 1892," with exposition buildings; "Columbian Exposition 1893," with a representation of the Fishery Building, made by Stern Brothers & Company, New York; St. Louis World's Fair, 1904, with buffalo, Indians, canoe, signal fire, Conestoga wagon, locomotive engine, trees and the setting sun in the west. Simons made the original, which may have had lettering. Fifty years later it made replicas which are handsome, without lettering, and of heavy weight.

Souvenir thimbles are still made and these recent ones are worth collecting. A thimble with scenes of the exposition at Philadelphia, 1926, marked "Sesqui-Centennial 1776–Philadelphia–1926" was made by Simons. "Century of Progress, Chicago–1934," was also made by Simons. There were souvenir thimbles of: Florida in raised letters with an alligator, made by Ketcham & McDougall, New York; Hawaii with seal, 1949; Maniton (a spa in Colorado) ; Palm Springs (Florida) with palm trees, etc.; Portland, Oregon, 1927; "Salem (Mass.) 1692" in raised letters with quarter moon, witch, cat and three pins, made by Ketcham & McDougall; "St. Augustine, Fla., Settled 1565," in raised letters with a coat of arms, made by Ketcham & McDougall; "Washington, D. C.," with a picture of the White House.

Souvenir thimbles of historic locations, buildings and parks were numerous. One had an enameled shield with red and white stripes in the lower part and a blue ground with white stars in the upper part, on an engraved band with an anchor on each side. This thimble came in a wooden case on the lid of which there is a transfer print of Bunker Hill Monument. It was made by Goldsmith, Stern & Company, New York, but the case is similar to other souvenir items made in Scotland. Others were: "Homestead Hot Springs, Va.," with a representation of the hotel, made by Ketcham & McDougall; "Merced General Hosp., Merced, Calif.," with a representation of the hospital; "Battle of Plattsburgh, September 11, 1814, Lake Champlain," with lake and ships, made by Ketcham & McDougall; "Rocky Mountain—Big Horn Sheep from Grand Lake—Colorado"; one with its entire sides enameled pictured the White House and the Washington Monument; and another showed Yellowstone Park, with a seal.

There are innumerable foreign souvenirs. Silver thimbles with enameled bands—sometimes with just as enameled shield —on which there would be the name of the city with perhaps a typical symbol: Venice with a gondola on a canal; Rome with the Colosseum; Paris with the Eiffel Tower; Lourdes with the shrine; Australia with a kangaroo; Switzerland with William Tell's Chapel, etc.

The English made a great many commemorative thimbles, including those featuring the following events: The engagement of Victoria and Albert, with pictures in oval with rose-and-thistle decoration; Queen Victoria "Crowned June 28, 1835," with crown and rose-and-thistle decoration; "Prince Royal Born at Buckingham Palace, November 21st, 1840," picture of Queen and angel with infant prince; "Jubilee 1887"; "The Diamond Jubilee of Queen Victoria, 1837–1897"; "Silver Jubilee 1910–1935, King George V Queen Mary," with crown; "E.R. 1953," coronation of Queen Elizabeth, horses and coach, London Bridge and angel with trumpet. "Exhibitions of All Nations 1851," picture of Glass Palace—enameled band; "International Exhibition 1862," picture of Victoria and Albert Museum—enameled band.

There are carved bog-oak thimbles from Erin with shamrocks and sometimes the name "Killarney," and onyx thimbles from Mexico with colored flowers and "Pueblo." Some of these have semiprecious stones set in their tops. Modern thimbles are set with a synthetic stone which has the appearance of plastic.

SEWING BIRDS

Although many people have never heard of sewing birds, they are defined in both the *Century Dictionary* and the third *Webster's International*. The *Century* gives the fullest definition: "A clamp used by women to hold fabrics in position for stitching by hand. The bird is screwed to the edge of the table, and its beak which closes on a spring can be opened by a lever actuated by the tail to hold material." In English eighteenth-century catalogues, sewing birds came under the heading of "steel toys" and were called "Ladies' Netting Vises." In the earlier vises, the embroidery or netting was held by a small hook, later spring jaws held the material and a pincushion and bobbin spindle were often added.

The early ones have a cushion, and the vises are decorated with pierced work, facets and small diamond-cut studs which add richness and are an example of the steelcutter's art. These were also made in cast brass and cast iron in the nineteenth century. Dolphins, birds and other figures were added later. The popular English and European design was a dolphin. The clamp was ornamented with an acanthus leaf. These designs later included a shell above the dolphin, and this sometimes held a naked child or *amorino* standing or riding a dolphin, and a caryatid.

Brass sewing bird, wings extended. Marked: "Norton's Improved Patent Applied for May, 1853."
COURTESY SMITHSONIAN INSTITUTION.

Sewing bird, silver-plated brass. Variation of clamp patented by Julius E. Merriman, July 26, 1853.
COURTESY SMITHSONIAN INSTITUTION.

Sewing butterfly, silver-plated brass. Variation of clamp patented by John Lane, 1853. COURTESY SMITHSONIAN INSTITUTION.

Sewing bird in form of dog. Silver-plated brass. Second half, 19th century. COURTESY SMITHSONIAN INSTITUTION.

Other sewing-bird designs include a stag, a frog, a butterfly, a box and even a dog. Varieties of birds include tomtits, miniature hummingbirds, hens, birds of paradise, duckhead birds and eagles. There were also early sewing birds of turned wood made in various designs and curiously like some pieces of modern wood sculpture. Other wooden designs were of a simple box with a blue stenciled design.

The sewing bird does not seem to have been used extensively in America until the middle of the nineteenth century, but by that time the popular form was the bird. They were known as sewing birds, and this design was the one most often used by American manufacturers. Sewing birds were sold in toy and novelty shops, and today one would find them in the notion department.

In the Hartford *Times,* June 5, 1852, Elihu Geer advertised: "Ladies Sewing Birds. The latest invented and most useful article for the use of ladies that can be found." The accompanying cut pictured two ladies sitting by a table, one using the sewing bird and the other holding her embroidery in her hand. In the Hartford *Calendar,* December 18, 1852, Elihu Geer again advertised: "Sewing Birds, 6 kinds, from 37½ to 62½ cts.," and in December 1853, his ad read: "Sewing birds 12 different kinds."

There were no descriptions of these birds, but we know from various collections assembled in the last few years that in addition to the numerous designs there were also many differences in mechanical workings. Some birds were made to hold the material in their bills, others held it under the bill, and still others grasped it with their bodies. Also the dies and patterns of the feathers varied, and some birds were designed with open wings. Other birds had a cushion on an arm of the

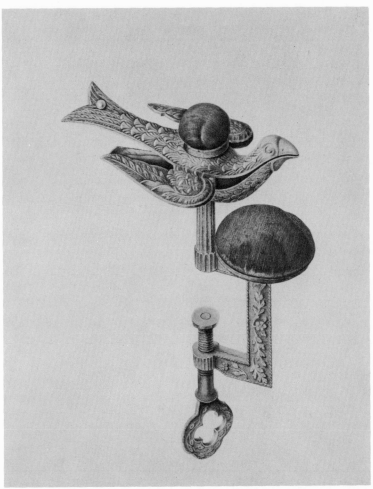

Sewing bird with feather design on body and open wings. Cast-and-stamped brass plated with silver. COURTESY INDEX OF AMERICAN DESIGN.

vise, while some carried a small cushion in their backs, to hold the emery for needle sharpening.

From 1853, American sewing birds were protected by patents. Allen Gerould and John H. Ward of Middletown, Connecticut, took out a patent in this year; their bird held the material with its body. A. P. Bailey of Middletown took out a patent in 1854; the Bailey bird held the material in its bill and it had no cushion or emery. John North of Middletown took out his patent in 1855; on this bird there is a small cup that holds a pincushion. While most of the sewing birds seem to have been made in Connecticut, De Coven of Brunswick, Maine, also made sewing birds, and in fact they were made in the novelty departments of most of the steel companies of America.

In all, there are over 160 types and varieties of sewing birds. Many are marked with the patent date but few with the maker's name.

Victorian Fancy Glass Baskets and Rose Bowls

LATE VICTORIAN tablewares and decorative glasswares were made in fancy forms and color effects which represent a high degree of technical achievement, if not always artistic worth. These fancy wares were made for popular appeal, pleased the Late Victorians, and have continued in popularity today. Not only were their names—frosted, shaded, pearled, opalescent, spangled, spattered and iridescent—romantic, but their forms were often as fanciful as the ruffled styles of Victorian clothes. The rims were crimped and ruffled, and the handles were braided or twisted into loveknots or decorated with applied flowers.

Baskets in every form were a delight to Victorian ladies, and the glass basket with handle and crimped rim was a particular favorite. The rose bowl, made for the storage of rose petals, was also dear to the hearts of the sentimental. These two forms were made in most of the popular glassware of the late nineteenth century, and a collection of baskets or rose bowls in the various fancy glasswares is not only attractive but will be a record of the era.

Although the shapes of baskets and rose bowls are varied

and fanciful, perhaps their greatest appeal is their color. Color is the dominant characteristic of fancy glass. Much of it is delicate, such as the pinks and blues and bittersweet shades of satin glass. Then there are the deep reds of peachblow and amberina, the browns of tortoise shell and agate, and the gold, blue and greens of iridescent glass. A short outline of Victorian fancy glass types will be of assistance to the collector of baskets and rose bowls.

The best known of these are Peachblow, Amberina, Burmese, Agata, Pomona, Spangled, Hobnail and Mother-of-pearl or Satin glass. Peachblow, one of the most beautiful of the shaded wares, was made at three glass companies. That made at the Mount Washington Glass Company in New Bedford, Massachusetts, is delicate in coloring, from rose-pink to pale blue. That made by Hobbs, Brockunier & Company at Wheeling, West Virginia, shades from rosy red to greenish yellow and has a milk-white lining. The Peachblow of the New England Glass Company at Cambridge, Massachusetts, is called Wild Rose and shades from creamy white to deep rose. This company also made Agata, a variation of Peachblow, which has a mottled, glossy effect in shades of white to rose.

Amberina and Burmese are also shaded wares. Amberina is transparent and thus seems lighter and gayer; its colors shade from pale amber yellow to rich ruby. The majority of the many ornamental and table pieces were patterned in molds in designs of expanded diamonds or ogivals, inverted thumbprint or swirled ribbing. There are rare Amberina baskets in inverted thumbprint and swirled patterns with crimpled rim tops. After 1888, Amberina was made by the Libbey Glass Company of Toledo, Ohio, and marked "Libbey—made in U.S.A." Burmese, like Peachblow, is opaque

Spangled glass baskets with twisted and overshot handles. Rainbow mother-of-pearl Satin-glass rose bowl, diamond quilted pattern.

COURTESY BENNINGTON MUSEUM, BENNINGTON, VT.

PHOTO LLOYD STUDIO.

and has a velvety surface, either dull or glossy. The decoration is painted or molded in patterns such as hobnail or applied florals. Burmese was made in a large variety of decorative glassware and tablewares.

All of these types of glassware get their two-toned color effects by the addition of gold and other metals to the glass mix. Pomona glass was a clear brown which was treated with etching, tinting or staining in shades of amber. It was often decorated with garlands of pale blue-stained cornflowers. Other patterns were fern leaves, pansies, and berries and vines. Sometimes pieces are pattern molded in a waffle design. Other types of frosted glass have crackled or rough overshot surfaces.

Another type of late-nineteenth-century glass was spattered with several colors so that it looked like tortoise shell or agate. Spatter or End-of-day glass and Spangleware were of this type. Glass baskets were one of the most popular shapes of Spangled glass. These baskets with ruffled rims and fancy handles come in various sizes, shapes and colors. Some have applied flowers and leaves. Another name given to Spangled glass is Vasa Murrhina.

Opalescent glass also had a special appeal to Victorians. The best known was called Dewdrop or Opalescent Dewdrop. It was perfected by the Hobbs Brockunier Company of Wheeling, West Virginia, and first came on the market in 1886. Today it is known by the popular name of hobnail, which relates to its appearance. It was first patterned in the mold, then expanded and formed by hand. It comes in a wide range of forms and colors. Some opalescent glass is solid opalescent all the way through; other pieces are shaded to form a colored border or raised in patterns and borders;

others are swirl striped. The variations come from hand manipulation. Onyx glass is cream color with a daisy-and-leaf pattern in metallic luster. It also comes in opalescent amber or pink with a trim in a deeper tone of the same color. An interesting basket with crimpled rim and braided handle is in the Mansion Museum, Oglebay Institute, Wheeling, West Virginia.

Mother-of-pearl or Satin glass was blown in a pattern mold. Most Satin glass has a lining of white glass and a colored coating. The surface was subjected to an acid vapor which gave it the satin finish. Some pearl wares are distinguished by their patterns of diamonds, herringbone or swirls. Others are of plain color with a silky satin finish and delicate shading of colors. The rarest colors are robin's-egg blue, bittersweet and rainbow stripes of blue, pink and yellow.

More rose bowls were made of Satin glass than of any other type. They were made in four sizes and were plain, painted or enameled. The glass was usually in rainbow colorings, yellow shading to white, dark rose or pink to white, and blue to white. Any other colors were rare. Many of the rose bowls were striped or diamond quilted. They ranged from 3″ to 6″ in height. A 2″ bowl in blue is rare. The tops of the bowls were crimped, and some had flower-and-leaf applied decoration.

Baskets were also made in Satin glass with ornate white handles and feet. The basket itself might be striped or blue to white with applied flower-and-leaf decoration. An amber basket with bell-shaped flowers in opaque white is rare. There is also a pink Satin-glass basket in hobnail design. A blue basket with canary yellow lining and a clear glass handle is especially beautiful, as are any of those in that color.

Spangled glass basket. American, 19th century. COURTESY HENRY FORD MUSEUM.

Metalized or iridescent glass was first made in America by Louis Tiffany and Frederick Carder at Corning, New York. Tiffany's Favrille and Carder's Aurene were high-quality products and never cheap. Many pieces are one of a kind. Tiffany's Favrille was made in fanciful and imaginative blown shapes, and the designs were taken from flowers and birds. Flower forms included gladioli, morning glory, iris and leaf-and-vine patterns. The peacock feather was also a favorite motif. Tiffany glass shows Persian and Oriental influence, but the tops of vases often had the favorite Victorian crimpled rim. Tiffany also made a large amount of tablewares in a variety of shapes, colors and designs. Most of Carder's Aurene glass has a smooth iridescent surface and excellent blown form. There are ridges, grooves and crimped edges, but no pressed-surface patterns. The thin coating of metal blown on the glass gave it iridescence, and the colors sometimes have beautiful rose-and-yellow tints, like a sunset. The shapes of the tinted and twisted forms are especially interesting in contrast to Favrille, which puts more emphasis on design and color. There are baskets of Aurene glass.

The easy, cheap way to produce iridescent glassware is by spraying a coating of metallic chloride over the glass object while it is still hot. The cheap Carnival pressed glass with an iridescent glow was made this way. It was manufactured in great quantities at several American factories. Carnival glass was made in many decorative patterns, including Peacock and Urn, Grape, Cherry, Peach and Singing Birds, as well as a geometric grapevine lattice. Orange bowls and nappies with scrolled feet and crimped tops had the same appeal as the earlier baskets. Rose bowls were also crimped, footed, and embossed with fruit or flower designs. They were available

Mother-of-pearl rose bowl with white cameo decoration on blue ground. A. CHRISTIAN REVI COLLECTION.

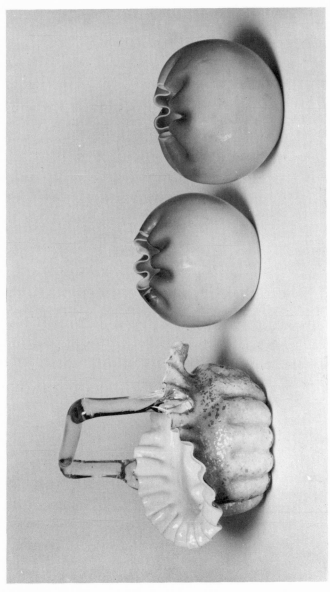

Gold-flecked glass basket, probably made at Hobbs, Brockunier. Two Satin-glass rose bowls. COURTESY SMITHSONIAN INSTITUTION.

in royal blue, amethyst, gold, ruby, rainbow and opal with sparkling metallic luster.

Although Carnival glass was cheap and garish, it touched the fancy of many people. Collectors have turned to it today because it is available in large quantities. Also, it is inexpensive and has never been reproduced. Carnival glass is also called taffeta, nancy and luster. It was made in hundreds of patterns and sold at carnivals and in ten-cent stores as late as 1920. It has been found with only one mark, "N," underlined or within a circle, which is the mark of Harry Northwood. The first iridescent glass that Northwood made in about 1900 was blown, then iridized. There are rare red vases from this period, but the mass production was pressed.

Patterns advertised in the 1910 catalogue were "Golden Iris," "Royal Purple," "Venetian Blue," "Venetian Red" and "Venetian Green." "Opaline Brocade" came in four colors, including pink. "Intaglio" was made in ivory and gold and green and gold. Because of its marking, Northwood has become the most highly prized of the carnivalwares, but this glass was also made by several other factories. Carnival glass has gained in popularity in the last few years and as a result, the price is going up. Reds and pastels are the rarest colors.

All these fancy glasswares are decorative, and a collection in a dining-room cupboard could be made the starting point for the room's decoration. To me, they have the appeal of a traditional Southern belle—delicate, romantic and sentimental—a little affected but altogether charming.

Victorian Pottery Jugs

JUGS DECORATED with relief patterns cast in the mold were popular in England and America from the 1840's. These jugs were usually 7″ or 8″ high and had an upward flaring lip and a round, low weighted body set on a solid foot. The handle, although usually decorative, was designed for service. The round, squat shape was the most typically Victorian, but in 1847, T & R Boote registered "a new shape for jugs." This was a straight-sided form without a base. A convolvulus jug and a jug with a boy bird-nesting were made on this form. These jugs were probably used for beer, since the subject matter of many of the designs suggests conviviality.

The jugs were made in various materials from brown salt-glaze stoneware to white Parian, but generally they were in fine putty-colored stoneware. They were not glazed and were usually buff or drab in color. Sometimes the relief or the ground was in color.

Copeland, Minton, Samuel Alcock and many less-known potters made these jugs. Although the greater number of them were made in the middle of the nineteenth century, Wedgwood shows a leafage jug and a Gothic design on a page of dry-body shapes in his catalogue of 1817. The leafage jug was made in drab, cane or white, and the Gothic "in one color as drab, cane or white, and in 2 colors as cane and blue or drab and white." Wedgwood made a jug with a relief of "Bacchanalian Boys" which also influenced later jug designs.

The designs of these relief-decorated stoneware jugs are as typically Victorian as the shapes, and they fall into several categories which directly relate to the life of Victorian times. There are naturalistic plant-and-flower designs in running patterns such as the Hop, Grape, Lily, Oak, Convolvulus and the Bird-nesting Boy. There were also log and vegetable forms such as the Cauliflower, Pineapple and Corn, as well as Minton's Acorn, made in 1875, and Wedgwood's Wicker in 1880.

The Gothic designs were particularly popular and are one of the most interesting categories. The Wedgwood Gothic jug had classical figures. Ridgway, Son & Company brought out a white stoneware jug in 1840 which had jousting figures within Gothic borders. But the best-known Gothic jug has figures of the Apostles set in Gothic niches. It has a rectangular body and was brought out by Charles Meigh in 1842. In 1846, T. J. & J. Mayer also manufactured a white stoneware jug with Apostle figures in niches, and in 1848, T. & R. Boote made a jug with a scene of the infant Samuel set in a Gothic framework. In the *Art Journal* catalogue of the 1851 Exposition, Charles Meigh & Son illustrated a Gothic jug with the Virgin and Child and St. John set under a Gothic canopy. The handle has the form of the framework of a Gothic window. The Gothic theme continued in popularity. In the Paris Exhibition of 1855, Cork and Edge advertised an Apostles jug, and in 1859, Samuel Alcock advertised a Daniel-in-the-lion's-den set in Gothic borders.

Classical designs, although not as popular, included a jug

Stoneware jug with hunting scene, cream with blue-enamel band. English, early 19th century. COURTESY METROPOLITAN MUSEUM OF ART.

Apostle jug, buff stoneware. Charles Meigh, 1842. COURTESY METROPOLITAN MUSEUM OF ART.

Jug, Parian ware. English, 19th century. COURTESY METROPOLITAN MUSEUM OF ART.

Parian porcelain pitcher with scene of the Good Samaritan. Samuel Alcock & Co. COLLECTION OF MRS. IRVING SNYDER. GEORGE AQUINO PHOTO.

with dancing figures adapted from Poussin's "Bacchanalian Dance," the popular Silenus jug made by Minton's, a Graces jug and a classical combat scene. There were also several jugs with cherubs—*amorini*—with or without wings, playing with garlands. One of the most elaborate beer jugs was designed by John Bell and put on the market by Felix Summerly. It was a vertical design of hop arbors with figures of men and women gathering the hops and putting them in a basket. A nude figure upheld the lip of the jug, and another sat at the joining of the rustic handle. An *amorino* sat between a bundle of hops as a finial on the cover.

Perhaps the most popular type of design was the sporting or drinking scene, and there were many jugs illustrating the stag hunt. Wedgwood produced a hunt jug with horses and hounds against a background of country landscape in 1800. It was 5″ high, was molded, and had a molded fluting around the base. The Boston *Daily Advertiser* on January 19th, 1816, featured hunting jugs.

Drinking scenes included the W. Ridgway jug with scenes from *Tam O'Shanter*, a Bacchanal by Cork & Edge with a man sitting on a beer keg, and a Hop jug made by Minton's. Other genre scenes included gypsies, babes in the wood and a toby jug. There were also a few rare jugs with documentary scenes such as Minton's Coach and Railway illustrated in the *Journal of Design and Manufactures* in 1849; Assyrian excavations by Ridgway in 1851; the Crimean War jug in 1856; and the Indian Mutiny in 1858. There is a Victoria-and-Albert jug, and three Prince Albert jugs were brought out after his death in 1861. There is a commemorative jug with a bust of the Emperor Napoleon III set within a patriotic framework of a wreath, flags and eagles.

For the American market, Wedgwood also brought out a Centennial jug in 1876, with busts of Washington and Lincoln. In 1853, after Harriet Beecher Stowe's *Uncle Tom's Cabin* became popular in England, Ridgway produced a series of jugs with scenes from the book. They are of grayish-green stoneware, and the top of the handle is a figure of Uncle Tom with his hands clasped in prayer. The jug is marked on the base: "Published by Ridgway & Abingdon, January 1, 1853."

All of these jugs are easily identified by the maker's mark on the base, and most of them also have the registry marks which give the year, month and day. This makes for satisfactory collecting, since you can be sure of what you have. Also, the jugs were made in great quantities, so that many have survived and can thus be purchased at reasonable prices. Until recently they have been neglected, so there has been no reason to reproduce them, although those in museums were acquired some thirty years ago.

Many of these stoneware pitchers were exported to America and their influence is seen in American ceramic design after the 1850's. It is especially noticeable in the products of Norton & Fenton at Bennington, Vermont. Although Bennington made no stoneware jugs of this sort, it was influenced by the shapes and designs, and many of the designs on Bennington Parian and Rockingham pitchers, such as "Lily Pond," "Love and War," "The Good Samaritan," "Paul and Virginia" and "Snowdrop," are exact copies of their English forerunners.

The famous Bennington hound-handled jugs had hunting and foliage designs related to the English jugs, but their shapes were not Victorian. However, the Parian jugs take on the Victorian shape and the cherub-and-grape pattern in

Parian white or blue and white duplicated a design made by Wedgwood. The Parian cornhusk pattern, although distinctly American, is Victorian in spirit.

Although the pottery jug is a good field for the amateur collector, the English jugs are much less expensive and more available than the American, for anything American is in more demand today. The interest has now turned to the Victorian, but the wise collector will look to late Victorian and beyond if he wants to get any bargains.

REGISTRY MARKS

From 1842 to 1883, when the British Patent Office employed a registry mark on English manufactured goods. Wedgwood used the mark in addition to the trademark—along with other manufacturers—which indicated that the design was registered in the British Patent Office. When this mark appears, it is possible to tell the exact year, month and date of an object by using the following table.

INDEX TO THE LETTERS FOR EACH MONTH AND YEAR FROM 1842 TO 1867

YEAR		MONTH			
1842	X	January	C		CLASS
1843	H	February	G		YEAR
1844	C	March 1845	W		
1845	A	April	H		
1846	I	May	E	MONTH	DAY
1847	F	June	M		
1848	U	July	I		
1849	S	August	R		
1850	V	September	D		
1851	P	October	B		PARCEL
1852	D	November	K		
1853	Y	December	A		MAY 23, 1842
1854	J				
1855	E				
1856	L				
1857	K				
1858	B				
1859	M				
1860	Z				
1861	R	Letter R used from 1st to 19th September, 1857			
1862	O	December, 1860, Letter K used.			
1863	G				
1864	N				
1865	W				
1866	Q				
1867	T				

INDEX TO THE LETTERS FOR EACH MONTH AND YEAR FROM 1868 (WHEN REGISTRY MARK CHANGED) TO 1883

YEAR		MONTH			
		January	C	DATE	CLASS
1868	X	February	G		
1869	H	March	W		
1870	C	April	H		
1871	A	May	E	PARCEL	YEAR
1872	I	June	M		
1873	F	July	I		
1874	U	August	R		
1875	S	September	D		
1876	V	October	B		MONTH
1877	P	November	K		
1878	D	December	A		1ST JANUARY 1869
1879	Y				
1880	J				
1881	E				
1882	L				
1883	K				

Appendices

Appendices

Section I
COUNTRY ANTIQUES

1) *American Weather Vanes, Decoys and Eagles.*

FOR FURTHER READING
Barber, Joel D., *Wild Fowl Decoys.* Windward House, 1934.
Christensen, Erwin O., *Early American Wood Carving.* World
    Publishing Company, 1952.
Lipman, Jean, *American Folk Art in Wood, Metal and Stone.*
    New York, Pantheon, 1948.

WHERE TO SEE COLLECTIONS
Colonial Williamsburg, Va.
Newark Museum, Newark, N. J.
Henry Ford Museum, Dearborn, Mich.
Peabody Museum, Salem, Mass.
Shelburne Museum, Shelburne, Vt.

2) *American Hinges, Latches, Locks and Keys.*

FOR FURTHER READING
Sonn, Albert H., *Early American Wrought Iron.* Chas. Scrib-
    ners Sons, N. Y., 1928.

WHERE TO SEE COLLECTIONS
Yale Antique Lock Collection, Yale and Towne.
Iron Knockers and Locks, Hispanic Museum, New York City.
Doylestown Historical Museum, Doylestown, Pa.

3) *American Cake and Pudding Molds and Cooky Cutters.*

FOR FURTHER READING
Lichten, Frances, *The Folk Art of Rural Pennsylvania.* New
York, Charles Scribner Sons, 1946.

WHERE TO SEE COLLECTIONS
Landes Valley Museum, Lancaster, Pa.
Chester County Historical Society, West Chester, Pa.
Henry Ford Museum, Dearborn, Mich.
DuPont Museum, Winterthur, Del.

4) *Tinware—Plain, Punched and Grocery-Store Tin.*

FOR FURTHER READING
Gould, Mary Earle, *Antique Tin & Tole Ware—Its History
and Romance.* Tuttle, 1958.
New York Historical Society's Newspapers.

WHERE TO SEE COLLECTIONS
Mary Earle Gould Collection, Worcester, Mass.
Henry Ford Museum, Dearborn, Michigan.
Old Sturbridge Village, Old Sturbridge, Mass.
Shelburne Village, Shelburne, Vt.

SECTION II
ADVERTISING AMERICANA

1) *American Containers for Liquor, Medicine, etc.*

FOR FURTHER READING
McClinton, Katharine Morrison, *American Glass.* New York,
World Publishing Company.
McKearin, George and Helen, *American Glass.* New York,
Crown Publishers, 1941.

WHERE TO SEE COLLECTIONS
Henry Ford Museum, Dearborn, Michigan.
Shelburne Village, Shelburne, Vt.
Old Sturbridge Village, Old Sturbridge, Mass.

2) *Trade Paperweights.*

WHERE TO SEE COLLECTIONS

Bella C. Landauer Collection, New York Historical Society, New York City.

3) *Advertising Fans and Fancy Cardboard Souvenirs.*

4) *American Watch Papers.*

FOR FURTHER READING

Spear, Dorothea E., *American Watch Papers*, American Antiquarian Society.

WHERE TO SEE COLLECTIONS

American Antiquarian Society, Worcester, Mass.
Metropolitan Museum of Art, New York City.
Museum of the City of New York, New York City.
New York Historical Society, New York City.
New York University, New York City.

SECTION III
NURSERY ANTIQUES

1 and 2) *Childrens Rattles, Pottery Banks and Blow Birds; American Wooden Folk Toys.*

FOR FURTHER READING

Lipman, Jean, *American Folk Art in Wood, Metal and Stone.* New York, Pantheon, 1948.

WHERE TO SEE COLLECTIONS

Philadelphia Museum of Art, Philadelphia, Pa.
New York Historical Society, New York City.
Henry Ford Museum, Dearborn, Mich.
Shelburne Village, Shelburne, Vt.
Old Sudbury, Sudbury, Mass.
DuPont Museum, Winterthur, Del.
Essex Institute, Salem, Mass.

3) *English Pottery and Poreclain Dogs and Cats.*

FOR FURTHER READING

Connoisseur, vols. 10, 42, 59 and 64.

Philip Suval, Cats and Dogs, 49 E. 57, New York City.
Victoria and Albert Museum, London.
Needham's Antiques, Dogs.

SECTION IV
MINIATURES

1) *Silver Miniatures.*

FOR FURTHER READING
Catalogue of Loan Exhibition of Antique English Silver
Miniatures. James Robinson. Pennsylvania Museum
Bulletin, May 1934.

WHERE TO SEE COLLECTIONS
Boston Museum of Fine Arts.
Children's Museum, Hartford, Conn.
Essex Institute, (Large Collection). Salem, Mass.
Henry Ford Museum, Dearborn, Mich.
Metropolitan Museum of Art, New York City.
Minneapolis Institute of Arts.
Museum of the City of New York.
Museum of the Preservation of New England Antiquities,
Boston, Mass.
New York Historical Society, New York City.
Philadelphia Museum of Art.
Yale Gallery of Fine Arts.

2) *Pottery and Porcelain Miniatures.*

WHERE TO SEE COLLECTIONS
Metropolitan Museum of Art, New York City.
Museum of the City of New York.
Philip Suval, New York City.
D. M. and P. Manheim, New York City.

APPENDICES

3) *Miniatures in Tin, Pewter, Brass, Copper, Iron and Wood —Miniature Bric-a-Brac.*

WHERE TO SEE COLLECTIONS

Denver Art Museum, Denver, Colo.
Germanischer Museum, Nürnberg, Germany.
Helena Rubenstein Collection, New York City.
Museum of the City of New York.
Newark Museum, Newark, N. J.
Victoria and Albert Museum, London, England.

SECTION V
ANTIQUES FOR THE EPICURE

1) *Earthenware Teapots.*

FOR FURTHER READING

Barret, Richard Carter, *Bennington Pottery and Porcelain.* Crown Publishing Co., 1958.

Bemrose, G., *Nineteenth Century English Pottery and Porcelain.* 1951.

Blacker, J. F., *The ABC's of English Salt-Glaze Stoneware.* London, Stanley & Paul & Co., 1922.

Ceramic Art in Great Britain. London, Llewellyn Jewett Virtue & Co. Ltd., 1878.

Larsen, Elouise Baker, *American Views on Staffordshire.* New York, Doubleday, Doran & Co., 1939.

McClinton, Katharine Morrison, *Antique Collecting for Everyone.* McGraw-Hill, Inc., 1951, Bonanza Reprint, 1964.

McClinton, Katharine Morrison, *Handbook of Popular Antiques.* New York, Random House, 1945, Bonanza Reprint, 1963.

Mankowitz, Wolf, *Wedgwood.* London, B. T. Batsford, Ltd., 1953.

WHERE TO SEE COLLECTIONS

Metropolitan Museum of Art, New York City.

Newark Museum of Art, Newark, N. J.
Victoria and Albert Museum, London, England.

2) *Pottery Cow Creamers.*

FOR FURTHER READING

John, W. D., *Old English Lustre Pottery.* Newport-Mon,
England, R. H. Johns Ltd., 1951.
Nance, E. Morton, *Pottery and Porcelain of Swansea and
Nantgarw.* B. T. Batsford, Ltd., London, 1942.

WHERE TO SEE COLLECTIONS

Bennington Museum, Bennington, Vt.
Ginsberg & Levy, New York City.
New York Historical Society, New York City.
Philip Suval, New York City.
Wadsworth Atheneum, Hartford, Conn.

3) *Nineteenth-Century American Spoons and Souvenir
Spoons.*

FOR FURTHER READING

Currier, Ernest, *American Silversmiths.* Southworth-Anthoe-
sen Press, Portland, Maine, 1938.
Ensko, G. C., *American Silversmiths and Their Marks.* 1927–
1948—Privately Printed.

WHERE TO SEE COLLECTIONS

All antique shows.
New York Historical Society, New York City.
Smithsonian Institute, Washington, D. C.

4) *Viands in Pottery and Porcelain.*

WHERE TO SEE COLLECTIONS

Bayerishes National Museum, Munich, Germany.
Musée des Arts Décoratifs, Paris, France.
Victoria and Albert Museum, London, England.

SECTION VI
VICTORIANA

1) *Victorian Cardcases and Calling Cards.*

WHERE TO SEE COLLECTIONS

American Antiquarian Society, Worcester, Massachusetts.
Metropolitan Museum of Art, New York City.
New York Historical Society, New York City.
New York Public Library, New York City.

2) *Victorian Scissors, Thimbles and Sewing Birds.*

FOR FURTHER READING

Old Time New England. April, 1950.
The Spinning Wheel. April, October, 1953.
Hartford, Conn., newspapers, 1852–1853.

WHERE TO SEE COLLECTIONS

New York Historical Society, New York City.
Smithsonian Institute, Mabel W. Whiteley Collection, Washington, D. C.

3) *Victorian Fancy Glass Baskets and Rose Bowls.*

FOR FURTHER READING

Freeman, Larry, *Iridescent Glass.* Watkins Glenn, N. Y., Century House, 1964.
Koch, Robert and Tiffany, Louis C., *Rebel in Glass.* Crown, 1964.
Lee, Ruth Webb, *Nineteenth Century Art Glass.* Barrows, 1952.
McClinton, Katharine Morrison, *American Glass.* The World Publishing Co., New York, 1950.

WHERE TO SEE COLLECTIONS

Corning Museum of Glass, Corning, N. Y.
Smithsonian Institute, Washington, D. C.

4) *Victorian Pottery Jugs.*

FOR FURTHER READING

Lee, Albert, *Portraits in Pottery*. Boston, The Stratford Co., 1931.

Wakefield, Hugh, *Victorian Pottery*. New York, Thomas Nelson & Sons, 1962.

WHERE TO SEE COLLECTIONS

All antique shows.

Victoria and Albert Museum, London, England.

Index

INDEX